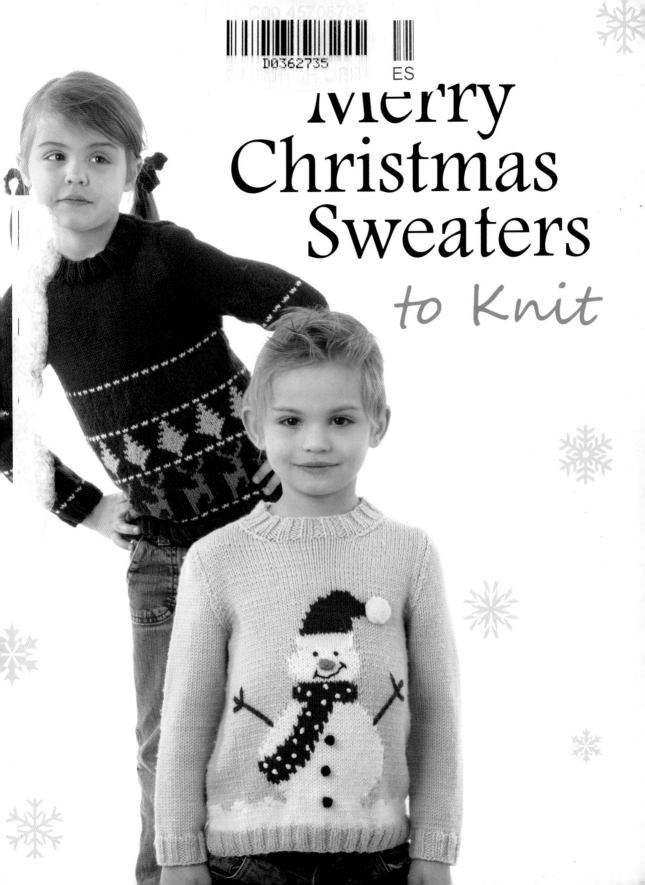

Merry Christmas Sweaters

to Knit

First published in Great Britain 2013

Search Press Limited
Wellwood, North Farm Road,
Tunbridge Wells, Kent TN2 3DR

Text copyright © Sue Stratford, 2013

Photographs by Paul Bricknell at
Search Press Studios

Photographs and design copyright
© Search Press Ltd, 2013

ISBN: 978-1-78221-011-5

Suppliers
If you have any difficulty obtaining any of the
materials and equipment mentioned in this book,
please visit the Search Press website:
www.searchpress.com

You are also invited to visit the author's website:
www.suestratford.co.uk

Printed in China

Dedication

This book is dedicated to my patient husband, Mark,
who always looks good in a Christmas sweater.

Acknowledgements

I most definitely could not have completed all the
knitting for this book within the tight time schedule
without help from some very special people. Thanks
especially to Jill, whose Fair Isle skills are out of
this world. Thanks also to Bekky, Susan, Heather,
Babs (who was chief bobble knitter) and Lucy (chief
bobble sewer). Special thanks also to Fiona. Finally,
thank you to the fabulous models who have brought
the sweaters to life: Lin Chan, Daniel Conway,
Faith and Andrew Edwards, Juan Hayward,
Marrianne Mercer, Liam O'Brien, Milly Randell,
Olivia Stephens, Lola and Poppy Stratford and
Oliver Whitfield.

Merry Christmas Sweaters
to Knit

Sue Stratford

SEARCH PRESS

Contents

THE MOTIFS 32

Introduction

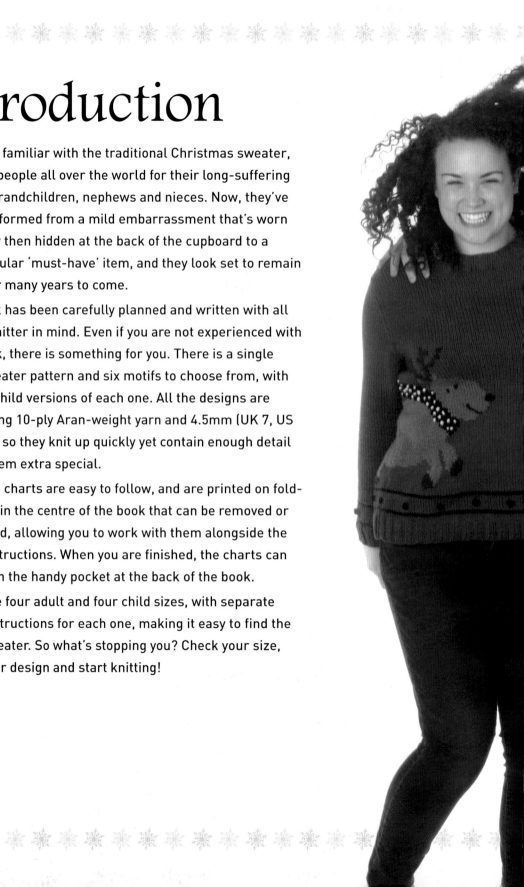

Everyone's familiar with the traditional Christmas sweater, knitted by people all over the world for their long-suffering children, grandchildren, nephews and nieces. Now, they've been transformed from a mild embarrassment that's worn for one day then hidden at the back of the cupboard to a hugely popular 'must-have' item, and they look set to remain popular for many years to come.

This book has been carefully planned and written with all levels of knitter in mind. Even if you are not experienced with colourwork, there is something for you. There is a single simple sweater pattern and six motifs to choose from, with adult and child versions of each one. All the designs are knitted using 10-ply Aran-weight yarn and 4.5mm (UK 7, US 7) needles, so they knit up quickly yet contain enough detail to make them extra special.

The large charts are easy to follow, and are printed on fold-out sheets in the centre of the book that can be removed or photocopied, allowing you to work with them alongside the written instructions. When you are finished, the charts can be stored in the handy pocket at the back of the book.

There are four adult and four child sizes, with separate pattern instructions for each one, making it easy to find the perfect sweater. So what's stopping you? Check your size, choose your design and start knitting!

How to use this book

1. Check your size and use the chart on page 64 to decide which size sweater to knit.

Before you choose your size you need to decide what kind of fit you want. Would you like a fitted look or a more casual over-sized sweater? If you use the chart giving the dimensions of each sweater, you can get exactly the fit you are looking for. Don't forget that sleeve and body length can be adjusted easily by working a few extra rows.

2. Choose your motif, using the pictures on pages 32–33.

You now need to choose which motif you would like on your sweater. Some of the designs, such as the Snowman, have a motif on the back as well as the front; others, such as the Santa Claus, only have a motif on the front. Several designs, such as the Reindeer, have a decorative edging around the hem and cuffs. The Christmas Pudding motif is knitted separately and stitched on to the front of a plain sweater – great if you are unfamiliar with intarsia techniques. The holly leaves can even be knitted separately and sewn on to the edging, cutting out the need for any colourwork completely. Try customising your sweater by mixing and matching motifs and borders. For example, why not knit the robin from the back of the Snowman sweater on to the back of the Santa Claus design to add a sweet surprise when you turn around!

3. Find the chart(s) for your chosen motif on the fold-out pages in the centre of the book.

The charts you need for each design are listed in the motifs section (pages 32–63). They can be cut out to allow you to use them alongside the pattern, and then stored in the pocket at the back of the book. If you find it easier, you can photocopy the chart, and then if you need to make notes while you are knitting you still have the original unmarked copy in the book. You might also like to trace over the red outline for your chosen size using a thick pen or highlighter.

4. Find the basic sweater pattern for your chosen size at the beginning of the book.

The basic sweater patterns are on pages 14–31. The rows on each pattern are numbered to match the charts so it is easy to work between the chart and the pattern. Before you start knitting, you may wish to familiarise yourself with the yarns, needles and basic techniques you need, including colourwork, using the information on pages 11–13.

5. Gather together the yarns, knitting needles and other items you need and get knitting!

The amounts of yarn you need for the basic sweater are provided on page 15, and the quantities for each of the motifs are given with the relevant instructions on pages 32–63. Remember to check your tension (gauge) first and familiarise yourself with the abbreviations used. These are provided on pages 14–15, and the abbreviations are also printed on the fold-out flap on the inside front cover.

Materials

You can use any 10-ply Aran-weight yarn to knit the sweaters. The patterns show the number of metres (yards) required to complete the basic sweater, making it easy for you to work out how many balls or skeins of your chosen yarn you need. Most ball bands show how many metres or yards are on the ball of yarn. The motifs pages provide details of the colours and quantities of yarns needed for the motifs themselves.

Just one size of knitting needle is used – 4.5mm (UK 7, US 7), or the adjusted size once you have completed your tension (gauge) swatch. You will also need a stitch holder to hold the stitches at the neckline on the front, and a darning needle is essential for the embroidery and making up. A row counter might also prove useful.

10

Techniques

Knitting with more than one colour of yarn

I have used both Fair Isle and intarsia techniques to knit the sweaters in this book, and have learnt a lot about both of these techniques in the process. If you are not confident with colourwork, I have designed a sweater just for you – the Christmas Pudding – which involves knitting the design separately then simply sewing it on.

Fair Isle

Fair Isle is a traditional method of knitting with two colours in which only a few stitches are worked in the contrasting colour. The yarn not being knitted is carried across the back of the work and looped over the working yarn every five to six stitches to ensure it stays close to the knitting. You need to make sure the loops are loose enough not to pull the work out of shape and distort the knitting, but not so loose that large loops appear at the back of the work.

There are several ways of knitting Fair Isle patterns. Experienced knitters can hold one colour of yarn in each hand, working one in the Continental way with the left hand and the other in the English style with the right hand. This prevents tangling and, if you love Fair Isle, it is a technique worth learning. Otherwise, just drop the yarn you have finished working with and pick up the new colour, leaving enough slack in the new yarn to prevent puckering – keeping the stitches spread out will help. To prevent tangling, always pick up the first colour over the second and then, when you change again, pick up the second colour under the first.

The reverse of the Nordic Fair Isle sweater, showing the Fair Isle technique.

The appearance of the design shown above, on the front of the sweater..

Intarsia

Intarsia is used when knitting a large block of contrasting colour. Instead of carrying the spare yarn across the back of the knitting, separate lengths of yarn are used for each colour, and the two colours are twisted around each other where they join to avoid holes forming. For example, on the snowman, knit the blue of the sweater, then drop the blue, start the cream for the body and then on the other side of the Snowman drop the cream and start a fresh ball of blue. Every time you change colour you must pass the old yarn colour over the new one and then lift the new one up from underneath so the colours are linked, like two people arm in arm. Otherwise you will simply be knitting completely separate sections.

The reverse of the Snowman sweater, showing the intarsia technique. It doesn't matter if the back looks a little messy – in fact, it's unavoidable if you are adding surface embroidery to your design. Try to be as neat as possible, though, and keep any threads carried across the back of the work as short and taut as possible, without puckering the work.

Making up
Blocking

Different knitters use different blocking techniques before sewing their garments together. I use steam blocking. Place a damp tea-towel over the knitting and use a steam iron to gently 'pat' the knitting and ease it into the correct size and shape. Pay particular attention to the edges to prevent rolling. Start with the front and back sweater pieces, making sure the side seams and shoulder seams match. Do the same with the sleeves, ensuring the underarm seams match. Use the measurements on page 64 to confirm the fit. Pin the knitting in place and allow to dry completely.

Mattress stitch

Mattress stitch is used to sew the parts of your sweater together. It gives a smooth, almost invisible seam and is worked between the edge stitch and the neighbouring stitch of each row.

Lay the two pieces of knitting side by side on a flat surface with the right sides facing up. Line up the seams you are joining accurately. Secure your yarn at the bottom of one of the pieces of knitting, take the needle across to the other piece and pass the yarn underneath the 'bar' between the first and second stitches of the first row. Take the needle back to the other side and repeat on the next row up. Continue working back and forth in this way until the whole seam has been worked, then fasten off the yarn. Keep the yarn fairly loose while you work and tighten it up every 4cm (1½in) or so, making sure the seam lies flat.

Knitting with two strands together

The sparkly white yarn used in several of the designs is finer than the 10-ply Aran yarn, so you will need to work with two strands at once to maintain the correct tension. The easiest way to do this is to find both ends of the ball and hold them together, knitting with both strands. Alternatively, you can roll your ball of yarn into two smaller balls.

Surface embroidery

To finish the motifs, some simple embroidery has been added, using a darning needle and the same yarn as that used for the knitting. Examples of the stitches used on the sweaters in this book are shown on the facing page.

French knots are useful for making dots on scarves and eyes. Simply bring your threaded needle through to the front of the work, wrap the yarn around it two or three times and take it back through in roughly the same position.

Stem stitch (shown below) has been used for fine lines, such as the mouths on the Reindeer and the Snowman.

Chain stitch is ideal for creating thicker lines, such as those used for the Snowman's arms and the vertical brick lines on Santa's chimney pot.

Swiss darning, also known as duplicate stitch, follows the shape of the knitted stocking stitches and looks as though it is part of the knitting. Fasten the yarn at the back of the work and bring the needle to the front at the base of the 'V'. Take it back through at the top of one arm of the 'V' and pull the yarn through so that it sits neatly over the top. Work the other side of the 'V' in the same way. It is a quick and easy way of adding the little stars to the top of the Winter Trees sweater.

Basic sweater patterns

Each of the following patterns is written for a specific size, and should be used in conjunction with the charts on the fold-out sheets in the centre of the book. Increases and decreases are specified row by row. This is because all the shapings are worked a stitch in from the edge of the knitting to obtain a straight, even line at the edges of the work. This makes it easier when making up and gives a very neat finish. This is especially evident on the neck shaping and makes the stitches for the neckband much easier to pick up. This method of shaping is known as fully fashioned shaping.

Tension (gauge)

The tension (gauge) used throughout this book is 18 stitches and 24 rows worked in SS = 10 x 10cm (4 x 4in) using 4.5mm (UK 7, US 7) knitting needles. If necessary, change to larger or smaller needles until you obtain the correct tension (gauge).

The sloping stitches you can see on either side of the neckline are where the shaping has been worked. The stitches at the front of the neck have been placed on a stitch holder and then worked.

All the abbreviations used in the patterns are provided below and on the fold-out flap on the inside front cover for easy reference. My preferred way for making a stitch (M1) is also explained here. It is worth using this method as it gives a really neat result and is virtually invisible. I now use this technique every time I need to increase in a pattern.

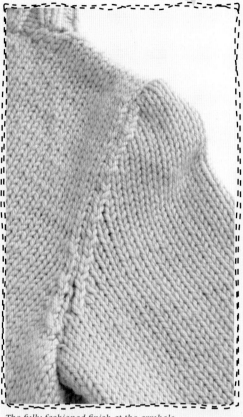

The fully fashioned finish at the armhole.

Abbreviations

beg	beginning
cont	continue
rem	remaining
rep	repeat
dec	decrease
inc	increase
K	knit
P	purl
SS	stocking stitch
st(s)	stitch(es)
K2tog	knit two stitches together
P2tog	purl two stitches together
K2togtbl	knit two stitches together through the back of the loops
P2togtbl	purl two stitches together through the back of the loops
sl1	slip one stitch to the right needle
ssK	slip two stitches knitwise, one at a time, pass the two slipped stitches back to the left needle, knit both together through the back of the loops
psso	pass slipped stitch over
M1	make a loop on your left-hand needle by wrapping the yarn towards you and slipping the resulting loop on to the right-hand needle. On the following row, knit or purl through the back of the stitch
Kfb	knit into front and back of the stitch, increasing by one stitch
Kfbf	knit into the front, back and front of the stitch, making two more stitches
RS	right side
WS	wrong side

Yarn quantities

The quantities below are for the basic sweaters; the yarn requirements for the motifs are provided on the relevant pages of the motifs section on pages 32–63. Note that both the metric and imperial quantities have been rounded up to the nearest ten to ensure you buy enough yarn to complete the sweater.

Adult

S	M	L	XL
900m	1000m	1100m	1250m
990yds	1100yds	1210yds	1370yds

Child

5–6	7–8	9–10	11–12
420m	500m	600m	700m
460yds	550yds	660yds	770yds

Adult: Small

Front

Using 4.5mm (UK 7, US 7) needles, cast on 92 sts.

Next row: (K2, P2), rep to end of row.

Rep this row a further 11 times.

Working from the Front Chart for your chosen motif, cont as follows:

Work in SS for 82 rows or until work measures 38cm (15in).

Cont in SS, working decreases as shown to shape armholes:

Row 83: Cast off 6 sts at beg of row [86 sts].

Row 84: Cast off 6 sts at beg of row [80 sts].

Row 85: K1, ssK, K to last 3 sts, K2tog, K1 [78 sts].

Row 86: P1, P2tog, P to last 3 sts, P2togtbl, P1 [76 sts].

Row 87: K1, ssK, K to last 3 sts, K2tog, K1 [74 sts].

Row 88: Purl.

Row 89: K1, ssK, K to last 3 sts, K2tog, K1 [72 sts].

Row 90: Purl.

Row 91: Knit.

Row 92: P1, P2tog, P to last 3 sts, P2togtbl, P1 [70 sts].

Row 93: Knit.

Row 94: Purl.

Row 95: K1, ssK, K to last 3 sts, K2tog, K1 [68 sts].

Row 96: Purl.

Row 97: Knit.

Row 98: Purl.

Row 99: Knit.

Row 100: Dec 1 st at each end of row [66 sts].

Cont with no further shaping until row 114 is complete.

Shape Front Neck as follows:

Row 115: K27, turn, leaving rem sts on a st holder. Cont working over these 27 sts.

Row 116: Cast off 2 sts at beg of row [25 sts].

Row 117: Knit.

Row 118: P1, P2tog, P to end of row [24 sts].

Row 119: K to last 3 sts, K2tog, K1 [23 sts].

Row 120: P1, P2tog, P to end of row [22 sts].

Row 121: K to last 3 sts, K2tog, K1 [21 sts].

Row 122: P1, P2tog, P to end of row [20 sts].

Row 123: Knit.

Row 124: P1, P2tog, P to end of row [19 sts].

Row 125: Knit.

Row 126: P1, P2tog, P to end of row [18 sts].

Row 127: Knit.

Row 128: P1, P2tog, P to end of row [17 sts].

Row 129: Knit.

Row 130: Purl.

Row 131: K to last 3 sts, K2tog, K1 [16 sts].

Row 132: Purl.

Row 133: Cast off 5 sts at beg of row [11 sts].

Row 134: Purl.

Row 135: Cast off 6 sts at beg of row [5 sts].

Row 136: Purl.

Row 137: Cast off rem 5 sts.

Place centre 12 sts on a st holder and, with RS facing, rejoin yarn to rem 27 sts. K to end of row.

Work second side as follows:

Row 116: Purl.

Row 117: Cast off 2 sts at beg of row [25 sts].

Row 118: P to last 3 sts, P2togtbl, P1 [24 sts].

Row 119: K1, ssK, K to end of row [23 sts].

Row 120: P to last 3 sts, P2togtbl, P1 [22 sts].

Row 121: K1, ssK, K to end of row [21 sts].

Row 122: P to last 3 sts, P2togtbl, P1 [20 sts].

Row 123: Knit.

Row 124: P to last 3 sts, P2togtbl, P1 [19 sts].

Row 125: Knit.

Row 126: P to last 3 sts, P2togtbl, P1 [18 sts].

Row 127: Knit.

Row 128: P to last 3 sts, P2togtbl, P1 [17 sts].

Row 129: Knit.

Row 130: Purl.

Row 131: K1, ssK, K to end of row [16 sts].

Row 132: Purl.

Row 133: Knit.

Row 134: Cast off 5 sts at beg of row [11 sts].

Row 135: Knit.

Row 136: Cast off 6 sts at beg of row [5 sts].

Row 137: Knit.

Row 138: Cast off rem 5 sts.

Back

Using 4.5mm (UK 7, US 7) needles, cast on 92 sts and work as for Front. Use the Back Chart for your chosen motif and follow the Front instructions for armhole shaping up to end of row 100 [66 sts].

With no further shaping, cont in SS until row 125 is complete.

Row 126: P29, cast off 8 sts and P to end of row. Cont over rem 29 sts, setting aside the first set of 29 sts to be completed later.

Row 127: Knit.

Row 128: Cast off 8 sts at beg of row [21 sts].

Row 129: K to last 3 sts, K2tog, K1 [20 sts].

Row 130: P1, P2tog, P to end of row [19 sts].

Row 131: Knit.

Row 132: Cast off 2 sts at beg of row [17 sts].

Row 133: Cast off 5 sts at beg of row, K to last 3 sts, K2tog, K1 [11 sts].

Row 134: Purl.

Row 135: Cast off 6 sts at beg of row, K to last 3 sts, K2tog, K1 [4 sts].

Row 136: Purl.

Row 137: Cast off rem 4 sts.

With RS facing, rejoin yarn to rem 29 sts and cont as follows:

Row 127: Knit.

Row 128: Purl.

Row 129: Cast off 8 sts at beg of row [21 sts].

Row 130: P to last 3 sts, P2togtbl, P1 [20 sts].

Row 131: K1, ssK, K to end of row [19 sts].

Row 132: Purl.

Row 133: Cast off 2 sts at beg of row [17 sts].

Row 134: Cast off 5 sts at beg of row, P to last 3 sts, P2togtbl, P1 [11 sts].

Row 135: Knit.

Row 136: Cast off 6 sts at beg of row, purl to last 3 sts, P2togtbl, P1 [4 sts].

Row 137: Knit.

Row 138: Cast off rem 4 sts.

Sleeves (make two)

Using 4.5mm (UK 7, US 7) needles, cast on 40 sts and work 12 rows in (K2, P2) rib, as for Front.

Cont in SS for 71 rows, working from Sleeve Chart if appropriate, and shaping as follows:

Inc 1 st at each end of rows 4, 11, 19, 26, 34, 41, 49, 56, 64 and 71 as follows: K1, M1, K to last st, M1, K1.

At the end of row 71 there will be 60 sts on the needle.

Cont in SS with no further shaping until row 90 is complete or until sleeve measures 41cm (16¼in).

Work sleeve-head shaping as follows:

Row 91: Cast off 5 sts at beg of row [55 sts].

Row 92: Cast off 5 sts at beg of row [50 sts].

Row 93: Cast off 2 sts at beg of row [48 sts].

Row 94: Cast off 2 sts at beg of row [46 sts].

Row 95: K1, ssK, K to last 3 sts, K2tog, K1 [44 sts].

Row 96: P1, P2tog, P to last 3 sts, P2togtbl, P1 [42 sts].

Row 97: Knit.

Row 98: P1, P2tog, P to last 3 sts, P2togtbl, P1 [40 sts].

Row 99: Knit.

Row 100: P1, P2tog, P to last 3 sts, P2togtbl, P1 [38 sts].

Row 101: Knit.

Row 102: P1, P2tog, P to last 3 sts, P2togtbl, P1 [36 sts].

Row 103: Knit.

Row 104: P1, P2tog, P to last 3 sts, P2togtbl, P1 [34 sts].

Row 105: Knit.

Row 106: Purl.

Row 107: Knit.

Row 108: P1, P2tog, P to last 3 sts, P2togtbl, P1 [32 sts].

Row 109: Knit.

Row 110: Purl.

Row 111: K1, ssK, K to last 3 sts, K2tog, K1 [30 sts].

Row 112: Purl.

Row 113: Knit.

Row 114: P1, P2tog, P to last 3 sts, P2togtbl, P1 [28 sts].

Row 115: Knit.

Row 116: Purl.

Row 117: K1, ssK, K to last 3 sts, K2tog, K1 [26 sts].

Row 118: Purl.

Row 119: Knit.

Row 120: P1, P2tog, P to last 3 sts, P2togtbl, P1 [24 sts].

Row 121: Knit.

Row 122: P1, P2tog, P to last 3 sts, P2togtbl, P1 [22 sts].

Row 123: Knit.

Row 124: Purl.

Row 125: K1, ssK, K to last 3 sts, K2tog, K1 [20 sts].

Row 126: P1, P2tog, P to last 3 sts, P2togtbl, P1 [18 sts].

Row 127: K1, ssK, K to last 3 sts, K2tog, K1 [16 sts].

Row 128: P1, P2tog, P to last 3 sts, P2togtbl, P1 [14 sts].

Row 129: K1, ssK, K to last 3 sts, K2tog, K1 [12 sts].

Row 130: Cast off rem 12 sts.

Making up

1. Join the right shoulder seam.

2. With RS facing and using 4.5mm (UK 7, US 7) needles, pick up and knit 19 sts along left front edge of neck shaping, knit across 12 sts on st holder and pick up and knit 19 sts along right front neck edge. Pick up and knit 19 sts to centre of back of neck and a further 19 sts to left back shoulder [88 sts].

3. Work 8 rows in (K2, P2) rib and cast off loosely and evenly in rib.

4. Join the left shoulder seam.

5. Lightly press or block all pieces of the sweater and sew the sleeves into the armholes, easing to fit.

6. Follow the finishing instructions for your chosen design, working any embroidery and details.

7. Sew the side seams and underarm seams, being careful to match any pattern.

8. Sew in all loose ends of yarn.

Adult: Medium

Front

Using 4.5mm (UK 7, US 7) needles, cast on 100 sts.

Next row: (K2, P2), rep to end of row.

Rep this row a further 11 times.

Working from the Front Chart for your chosen motif, cont as follows:

Work in SS for 84 rows or until work measures 39.5cm (15½in).

Cont in SS, working decreases as shown to shape armholes:

Row 85: Cast off 8 sts at beg of row [92 sts].

Row 86: Cast off 8 sts at beg of row [84 sts].

Row 87: K1, ssK, K to last 3 sts, K2tog, K1 [82 sts].

Row 88: P1, P2tog, P to last 3 sts, P2togtbl, P1 [80 sts].

Row 89: Knit.

Row 90: P1, P2tog, P to last 3 sts, P2togtbl, P1 [78 sts].

Row 91: Knit.

Row 92: P1, P2tog, P to last 3 sts, P2togtbl, P1 [76 sts].

Row 93: K1, ssK, K to last 3 sts, K2tog, K1 [74 sts].

Row 94: Purl.

Row 95: Knit.

Row 96: P1, P2tog, P to last 3 sts, P2togtbl, P1 [72 sts].

Row 97: Knit.

Row 98: Purl.

Row 99: Knit.

Row 100: P1, P2tog, P to last 3 sts, P2togtbl, P1 [70 sts].

Row 101: Knit.

Row 102: Purl.

Row 103: Knit.

Row 104: Purl.

Row 105: K1, ssK, K to last 3 sts, K2tog, K1 [68 sts].

Cont with no further shaping until row 122 is complete.

Shape Front Neck as follows:

Row 123: K27, turn, leaving rem sts on a st holder. Cont working over these 27 sts.

Row 124: Purl.

Row 125: Knit.

Row 126: Cast off 3 sts at beg of row [24 sts].

Row 127: Knit.

Row 128: Cast off 2 sts at beg of row [22 sts].

Row 129: Knit.

Row 130: Purl.

Row 131: K to last 3 sts, K2tog, K1 [21 sts].

Row 132: P1, P2tog, P to end of row [20 sts].

Row 133: Knit.

Row 134: P1, P2tog, P to end of row [19 sts].

Row 135: Knit.

Row 136: P1, P2tog, P to end of row [18 sts].

Row 137: Knit.

Row 138: Purl.

Row 139: K to last 3 sts, K2tog, K1 [17 sts].

Row 140: Purl.

Row 141: Cast off 6 sts at beg of row [11 sts].

Row 142: Purl.

Row 143: Cast off 6 sts at beg of row [5 sts].

Row 144: Purl.

Row 145: Cast off rem 5 sts.

Place centre 14 sts on a st holder and, with RS facing, rejoin yarn to rem 27 sts. K to end of row.

Work second side as follows:

Row 124: Purl.

Row 125: Cast off 3 sts at beg of row [24 sts].

Row 126: Purl.

Row 127: Cast off 2 sts at beg of row [22 sts].

Row 128: Purl.

Row 129: Knit.

Row 130: P to last 3 sts, P2togtbl, P1 [21 sts].

Row 131: K1, ssK, K to end of row [20 sts].

Row 132: Purl.

Row 133: K1, ssK, K to end of row [19 sts].

Row 134: Purl.

Row 135: K1, ssK, K to end of row (neck edge) [18 sts].

Row 136: Purl.

Row 137: Knit.

Row 138: P to last 3 sts, P2togtbl, P1 [17 sts].

Row 139: Knit.

Row 140: Cast off 6 sts at beg of row [11 sts].

Row 141: Knit.

Row 142: Cast off 6 sts at beg of row [5 sts].

Row 143: Knit.

Row 144: Cast off rem 5 sts.

Back

Using 4.5mm (UK 7, US 7) needles, cast on 100 sts and work as for Front. Use the Back Chart for your chosen motif and follow the instructions for Front armhole shaping up to end of row 105 [68 sts].

With no further shaping, cont in SS until row 133 is complete.

Row 134: P29, cast off 10 sts and P to end of row. Cont over rem 29 sts, setting aside the first set of 29 sts to be completed later.

Row 135: Knit.

Row 136: Cast off 7 sts at beg of row [22 sts].

Row 137: Knit.

Row 138: Cast off 3 sts at beg of row [19 sts].

Row 139: Cast off 6 sts at beg of row [13 sts].

Row 140: P1, P2tog, P to end of row [12 sts].

Row 141: Cast off 6 sts at beg of row [6 sts].

Row 142: P1, P2tog, P to end of row [5 sts].

Row 143: Cast off rem 5 sts.

With RS facing, rejoin yarn to rem 29 sts and cont as follows:

Row 135: Knit.

Row 136: Purl.

Row 137: Cast off 7 sts at beg of row [22 sts].

Row 138: Purl.

Row 139: Cast off 3 sts at beg of row [19 sts].

Row 140: Cast off 6 sts at beg of row [13 sts].

Row 141: K1, ssK, K to end of row [12 sts].

Row 142: Cast off 6 sts at beg of row [6 sts].

Row 143: K1, ssK, K to end of row [5 sts].

Row 144: Cast off rem 5 sts.

Sleeves (make two)

Using 4.5mm (UK 7, US 7) needles, cast on 44 sts and work 12 rows in (K2, P2) rib, as for Front.

Cont in SS for 86 rows, working from Sleeve Chart if appropriate, and shaping as follows:

Inc 1 st at each end of rows 3, 10, 17, 24, 31, 38, 44, 51, 58, 65, 72, 79 and 86 as follows: K1, M1, K to last st, M1, K1.

At the end of row 86 there will be 70 sts on the needle.

Cont in SS with no further shaping until row 92 is complete or until sleeve measures 41cm (16¼in).

Work sleeve-head shaping as follows:

Row 93: Cast off 5 sts at beg of row [65 sts].

Row 94: Cast off 5 sts at beg of the row [60 sts].

Row 95: Cast off 2 sts at beg of row [58 sts].

Row 96: Cast off 2 sts at beg of row [56 sts].

Row 97: K1, ssK, K to last 3 sts, K2tog, K1 [54 sts].

Row 98: P1, P2tog, P to last 3 sts, P2togtbl, P1 [52 sts].

Row 99: K1, ssK, K to last 3 sts, K2tog, K1 [50 sts].

Row 100: Purl.

Row 101: K1, ssK, K to last 3 sts, K2tog, K1 [48 sts].

Row 102: Purl.

Row 103: K1, ssK, K to last 3 sts, K2tog, K1 [46 sts].

Row 104: Purl.

Row 105: K1, ssK, K to last 3 sts, K2tog, K1 [44 sts].

Row 106: Purl.

Row 107: K1, ssK, K to last 3 sts, K2tog, K1 [42 sts].

Row 108: Purl.

Row 109: K1, ssK, K to last 3 sts, K2tog, K1 [40 sts].

Row 110: P1, P2tog, P to last 3 sts, P2togtbl, P1 [38 sts].

Row 111: K1, ssK, K to last 3 sts, K2tog, K1 [36 sts].

Row 112: Purl.

Row 113: K1, ssK, K to last 3 sts, K2tog, K1 [34 sts].

Row 114: Purl.

Row 115: Knit.

Row 116: Purl.

Row 117: K1, ssK, K to last 3 sts, K2tog, K1 [32 sts].

Row 118: Purl.

Row 119: K1, ssK, K to last 3 sts, K2tog, K1 [30 sts].

Row 120: P1, P2tog, P to last 3 sts, P2togtbl, P1 [28 sts].

Row 121: Knit.

Row 122: Purl.

Row 123: Knit.

Row 124: Purl.

Row 125: K1, ssK, K to last 3 sts, K2tog, K1 [26 sts].

Row 126: Purl.

Row 127: K1, ssK, K to last 3 sts, K2tog, K1 [24 sts].

Row 128: Purl.

Row 129: K1, ssK, K to last 3 sts, K2tog, K1 [22 sts].

Row 130: P1, P2tog, P to last 3 sts, P2togtbl, P1 [20 sts].

Row 131: Cast off 2 sts at beg of row [18 sts].

Row 132: Cast off 2 sts at beg of row [16 sts].

Row 133: Cast off rem 16 sts.

Making up

1. Join the right shoulder seam.

2. With RS facing and using 4.5mm (UK 7, US 7) needles, pick up and knit 19 sts along left front edge of neck shaping, knit across 14 sts on st holder and pick up and knit 19 sts along right front neck edge. Pick up and knit 20 sts to centre of back of neck and a further 20 sts to left back shoulder [92 sts].

3. Work 10 rows in (K2, P2) rib and cast off loosely and evenly in rib.

4. Join the left shoulder seam.

5. Lightly press or block all pieces of the sweater and sew the sleeves into the armholes, easing to fit.

6. Follow the finishing instructions for your chosen design, working any embroidery and details.

7. Sew the side seams and underarm seams, being careful to match any pattern.

8. Sew in all loose ends of yarn.

Adult: Large

Front

Using 4.5mm (UK 7, US 7) needles, cast on 108 sts.

Next row: (K2, P2), rep to end of row. Rep this row a further 11 times.

Working from the Front Chart for your chosen motif, cont as follows:

Work in SS for 88 rows or until work measures 39cm (15¼in).

Cont in SS, working decreases as shown to shape armholes:

Row 89: Cast off 5 sts at beg of row [103 sts].

Row 90: Cast off 5 sts at beg of row [98 sts].

Row 91: Cast off 4 sts at beg of row [94 sts].

Row 92: Cast off 4 sts at beg of row [90 sts].

Row 93: K1, ssK, K to last 3 sts, K2tog, K1 [88 sts].

Row 94: P1, P2tog, P to last 3 sts, P2togtbl [86 sts].

Row 95: K1, ssK, K to last 3 sts, K2tog, K1 [84 sts].

Row 96: P1, P2tog, P to last 3 sts, P2togtbl [82 sts].

Row 97: K1, ssK, K to last 3 sts, K2tog, K1 [80 sts].

Row 98: Purl.

Row 99: K1, ssK, K to last 3 sts, K2tog, K1 [78 sts].

Row 100: Purl.

Row 101: K1, ssK, K to last 3 sts, K2tog, K1 [76 sts].

Row 102: Purl.

Row 103: Knit.

Row 104: P1, P2tog, P to last 3 sts, P2togtbl [74 sts].

Row 105: Knit.

Row 106: P1, P2tog, P to last 3 sts, P2togtbl [72 sts].

Cont with no further shaping until row 128 is complete.

Shape Front Neck as follows:

Row 129: K30, turn, leaving rem sts on a st holder. Cont working over these 30 sts.

Row 130: Cast off 2 sts at beg of row [28 sts].

Row 131: Knit.

Row 132: P1, P2tog, P to end of row [27 sts].

Row 133: K to last 3 sts, K2tog, K1 [26 sts].

Row 134: P1, P2tog, P to end of row [25 sts].

Row 135: Knit.

Row 136: P1, P2tog, P to end of row [24 sts].

Row 137: K to last 3 sts, K2tog, K1 [23 sts].

Row 138: Purl.

Row 139: K to last 3 sts, K2tog, K1 [22 sts].

Row 140: Purl.

Row 141: K to last 3 sts, K2tog, K1 [21 sts].

Row 142: Purl.

Row 143: Knit.

Row 144: P1, P2tog, P to end of row [20 sts].

Row 145: Knit.

Row 146: Purl.

Row 147: Cast off 6 sts at beg of row, K to last 3 sts, K2tog, K1 [13 sts].

Row 148: Purl.

Row 149: Cast off 6 sts at beg of row [7 sts].

Row 150: Purl.

Row 151: Cast off rem 7 sts.

Place centre 12 sts on a st holder and, with RS facing, rejoin yarn to rem 30 sts. K to end of row.

Work second side as follows:

Row 130: Purl.

Row 131: Cast off 2 sts at beg of row [28 sts].

Row 132: P to last 3 sts, P2togtbl, P1 [27 sts].

Row 133: K1, ssK, K to end of row [26 sts].

Row 134: P to last 3 sts, P2togtbl, P1 [25 sts].

Row 135: Knit.

Row 136: P to last 3 sts, P2togtbl, P1 [24 sts].

Row 137: K1, ssK, K to end of row [23 sts].

Row 138: Purl.

Row 139: K1, ssK, K to end of row [22 sts].

Row 140: Purl.

Row 141: K1, ssK, K to end of row [21 sts].

Row 142: Purl.

Row 143: Knit.

Row 144: P to last 3 sts, P2togtbl, P1 [20 sts].

Row 145: Knit.

Row 146: Cast off 6 sts at beg of row [14 sts].

Row 147: K1, ssK, K to end of row [13 sts].

Row 148: Cast off 6 sts at beg of row [7 sts].

Row 149: Knit.

Row 150: Cast off rem 7 sts.

Back

Using 4.5mm (UK 7, US 7) needles, cast on 108 sts and work as for Front. Use the Back Chart for your chosen motif and follow the instructions for the Front armhole shaping up to end of row 106 [72 sts]. With no further shaping, cont in SS until row 139 is complete.

Row 140: P30, cast off 12 sts and P to end of row. Cont over rem 30 sts, setting aside the first set of 30 sts to be completed later.

Row 141: Knit.

Row 142: Cast off 6 sts at beg of row [24 sts].

Row 143: K to last 3 sts, K2tog, K1 [23 sts].

Row 144: P1, P2tog, P to end of row [22 sts].

Row 145: K to last 3 sts, K2tog, K1 [21 sts].

Row 146: P1, P2tog, P to end of row [20 sts].

Row 147: Cast off 6 sts at beg of row [14 sts].

Row 148: P1, P2tog, P to end of row [13 sts].

Row 149: Cast off 6 sts at beg of row [7 sts].

Row 150: Purl.

Row 151: Cast off rem 7 sts.

With RS facing, rejoin yarn to rem 30 sts and cont as follows:

Row 141: Knit.

Row 142: Purl.

Row 143: Cast off 6 sts at beg of row [24 sts].

Row 144: P to last 3 sts, P2tog, P1 [23 sts].

Row 145: K1, ssK, K to end of row [22 sts].

Row 146: Cast off 6 sts at beg of row, P to last 3 sts, P2tog, P1 [15 sts].

Row 147: K1, ssK, K to end of row [14 sts].

Row 148: Cast off 6 sts at beg of row [8 sts].

Row 149: K1, ssK, K to end of row [7 sts].

Row 150: Cast off rem 7 sts.

Sleeves (make two)

Using 4.5mm (UK 7, US 7) needles, cast on 46 sts and work 12 rows in (K2, P2) rib, as for Front.

Cont in SS for 86 rows, working from Sleeve Chart if appropriate, and shaping as follows:

Inc 1 st at each end of rows 3, 9, 15, 21, 27, 33, 39, 44, 50, 56, 62, 68, 74, 80 and 86 as follows: K1, M1, K to last st, M1, K1.

At the end of row 86 there will be 76 sts on the needle.

Cont in SS with no further shaping until row 96 is complete or until sleeve measures 41cm (16¼in).

Work sleeve-head shaping as follows:

Row 97: Cast off 4 sts at beg of row [72 sts].

Row 98: Cast off 4 sts at beg of row [68 sts].

Row 99: Cast off 3 sts at beg of row [65 sts].

Row 100: Cast off 3 sts at beg of row [62 sts].

Row 101: K1, ssK, K to last 3 sts, K2tog, K1 [60 sts].

Row 102: P1, P2tog, P to last 3 sts, P2togtbl, P1 [58 sts].

Row 103: K1, ssK, K to last 3 sts, K2tog, K1 [56 sts].

Row 104: P1, P2tog, P to last 3 sts, P2togtbl, P1 [54 sts].

Row 105: K1, ssK, K to last 3 sts, K2tog, K1 [52 sts].

Row 106: P1, P2tog, P to last 3 sts, P2togtbl, P1 [50 sts].

Row 107: K1, ssK, K to last 3 sts, K2tog, K1 [48 sts].

Row 108: Purl.

Row 109: K1, ssK, K to last 3 sts, K2tog, K1 [46 sts].

Row 110: Purl.

Row 111: Knit.

Row 112: Purl.

Row 113: Knit.

Row 114: Purl.

Row 115: K1, ssK, K to last 3 sts, K2tog, K1 [44 sts].

Row 116: Purl.

Row 117: Knit

Row 118: Purl.

Row 119: K1, ssK, K to last 3 sts, K2tog, K1 [42 sts].

Row 120: Purl.

Row 121: K1, ssK, K to last 3 sts, K2tog, K1 [40 sts].

Row 122: Purl.

Row 123: Knit.

Row 124: Purl.

Row 125: K1, ssK, K to last 3 sts, K2tog, K1 [38 sts].

Row 126: Purl.

Row 127: Knit.

Row 128: Purl.

Row 129: K1, ssK, K to last 3 sts, K2tog, K1 [36 sts].

Row 130: Purl.

Row 131: K1, ssK, K to last 3 sts, K2tog, K1 [34 sts].

Row 132: Purl.

Row 133: Knit.

Row 134: P1, P2tog, P to last 3 sts, P2togtbl, P1 [32 sts].

Row 135: Knit.

Row 136: Purl.

Row 137: K1, ssK, K to last 3 sts, K2tog, K1 [30 sts].

Row 138: Purl.

Row 139: K1, ssK, K to last 3 sts, K2tog, K1 [28 sts].

Row 140: P1, P2tog, P to last 3 sts, P2togtbl, P1 [26 sts].

Row 141: K1, ssK, K to last 3 sts, K2tog, K1 [24 sts].

Row 142: P1, P2tog, P to last 3 sts, P2togtbl, P1 [22 sts].

Row 143: Cast off 2 sts at beg of row [20 sts].

Row 144: Cast off 2 sts at beg of row [18 sts].

Row 145: Cast off 2 sts at beg of row [16 sts].

Row 146: Cast off 2 sts at beg of row [14 sts].

Row 147: Cast off rem 14 sts.

Making up

1. Join the right shoulder seam.

2. With RS facing and using 4.5mm (UK 7, US 7) needles, pick up and knit 19 sts along left front edge of neck shaping, knit across 12 sts on st holder and pick up and knit 19 sts along right front neck edge. Pick up and knit 21 sts to centre of back of neck and a further 21 sts to left back shoulder [92 sts].

3. Work 10 rows in (K2, P2) rib and cast off loosely and evenly in rib.

4. Join the left shoulder seam.

5. Lightly press or block all pieces of the sweater and sew the sleeves into the armholes, easing to fit.

6. Follow the finishing instructions for your chosen design, working any embroidery and details.

7. Sew the side seams and underarm seams, being careful to match any pattern.

8. Sew in all loose ends of yarn.

Adult: Extra Large

Front

Using 4.5mm (UK 7, US 7) needles, cast on 116 sts.

Next row: (K2, P2), rep to end of row.

Rep this row a further 11 times.

Working from the Front Chart for your chosen motif, cont as follows:

Work in SS for 90 rows or until work measures 42cm (16½in).

Cont in SS, working decreases as shown to shape armholes:

Row 91: Cast off 8 sts at beg of row [108 sts].

Row 92: Cast off 8 sts at beg of row [100 sts].

Row 93: Cast off 4 sts at beg of row [96 sts].

Row 94: Cast off 4 sts at beg of row [92 sts].

Row 95: K1, ssK, K to last 3 sts, K2tog, K1 [90 sts].

Row 96: P1, P2tog, P to last 3 sts, P2togtbl, P1 [88 sts].

Row 97: K1, ssK, K to last 3 sts, K2tog, K1 [86 sts].

Row 98: P1, P2tog, P to last 3 sts, P2togtbl, P1 [84 sts].

Row 99: K1, ssK, K to last 3 sts, K2tog, K1 [82 sts].

Row 100: P1, P2tog, P to last 3 sts, P2togtbl, P1 [80 sts].

Row 101: Knit.

Row 102: P1, P2tog, P to last 3 sts, P2togtbl, P1 [78 sts].

Row 103: Knit.

Row 104: P1, P2tog, P to last 3 sts, P2togtbl, P1 [76 sts].

Row 105: Knit.

Row 106: Purl.

Row 107: K1, ssK, K to last 3 sts, K2tog, K1 [74 sts].

Cont with no further shaping until row 130 is complete.

Shape Front Neck as follows:

Row 131: K30, turn, leaving rem sts on a st holder. Cont working over these 30 sts.

Row 132: Purl.

Row 133: Knit.

Row 134: Cast off 3 sts at beg of row [27 sts].

Row 135: Knit.

Row 136: P1, P2tog, P to end of row [26 sts].

Row 137: K to last 3 sts, K2tog, K1 [25 sts].

Row 138: Purl.

Row 139: K to last 3 sts, K2tog, K1 [24 sts].

Row 140: P1, P2tog, P to end of row [23 sts].

Row 141: K to last 3 sts, K2tog, K1 [22 sts].

Row 142: Purl.

Row 143: Knit.

Row 144: P1, P2tog, P to end of row [21 sts].

Row 145: Knit.

Row 146: Purl.

Row 147: K to last 3 sts, K2tog, K1 [20 sts].

Row 148: Purl.

Row 149: Cast off 6 sts at beg of row [14 sts].

Row 150: Purl.

Row 151: Cast off 7 sts at beg of row [7 sts].

Row 152: Purl.

Row 153: Cast off rem 7 sts.

Place centre 14 sts on a st holder and, with RS facing, rejoin yarn to rem 30 sts. K to end of row.

Work second side as follows:

Row 132: Purl.

Row 133: Cast off 3 sts at beg of row [27 sts].

Row 134: Purl.

Row 135: K1, ssK, K to end of row [26 sts].

Row 136: P to last 3 sts, P2togtbl, P1 [25 sts].

Row 137: Knit.

Row 138: P to last 3 sts, P2togtbl, P1 [24 sts].

Row 139: K1, ssK, K to end of row [23 sts].

Row 140: Purl.

Row 141: K1, ssK, K to end of row [22 sts].

Row 142: Purl.

Row 143: Knit.

Row 144: P to last 3 sts, P2togtbl, P1 [21 sts].

Row 145: Knit.

Row 146: Purl.

Row 147: K1, ssK, K to end of row [20 sts].

Row 148: Cast off 6 sts at beg of row [14 sts].

Row 149: Knit.

Row 150: Cast off 7 sts at beg of row [7 sts].

Row 151: Knit.

Row 152: Cast off rem 7 sts.

Back

Using 4.5mm (UK 7, US 7) needles, cast on 116 sts and work as for Front. Use the Back Chart for your chosen motif and follow the instructions for the Front armhole shaping up to end of row 107 [74 sts].

With no further shaping, cont in SS until row 144 is complete.

Row 145: K27, cast off 20 sts and K to end of row. Cont over rem 27 sts, setting aside the first set of 27 sts to be completed later.

Row 146: Purl.

Row 147: Cast off 4 sts at beg of row [23 sts].

Row 148: Cast off 6 sts at beg of row [17 sts].

Row 149: Cast off 2 sts at beg of row [15 sts].

Row 150: Cast off 7 sts at beg of row, P to last 3 sts, P2togtbl, P1 [7 sts].

Row 151: Knit.

Row 152: Cast off rem 7 sts.

With RS facing, rejoin yarn to rem 27 sts and cont as follows:

Row 146: Purl.

Row 147: Knit.

Row 148: Cast off 4 sts at beg of row [23 sts].

Row 149: Cast off 6 sts at beg of row [17 sts].

Row 150: Cast off 2 sts at beg of row [15 sts].

Row 151: Cast off 7 sts at beg of row, K to last 3 sts, K2tog, K1 [7 sts].

Row 152: Purl.

Row 153: Cast off rem 7 sts.

Sleeves (make two)

Using 4.5mm (UK 7, US 7) needles, cast on 48 sts and work 12 rows in (K2, P2) rib, as for Front.

Cont in SS for 87 rows, working from Sleeve Chart if appropriate, and shaping as follows:

Inc 1 st at each end of rows 3, 8, 13, 19, 24, 29, 34, 40, 45, 50, 56, 61, 66, 71, 77, 82 and 87 as follows: K1, M1, K to last st, M1, K1.

At the end of row 87 there will be 82 sts on the needle.

Cont in SS with no further shaping until row 100 is complete or until sleeve measures 42cm (16½in).

Work sleeve-head shaping as follows:

Row 101: Cast off 5 sts at beg of row [77 sts].

Row 102: Cast off 5 sts at beg of row [72 sts].

Row 103: Cast off 3 sts at beg of row [69 sts].

Row 104: Cast off 3 sts at beg of row [66 sts].

Row 105: Cast off 2 sts at beg of row [64 sts].

Row 106: Cast off 2 sts at beg of row [62 sts].

Row 107: K1, ssK, K to last 3 sts, K2tog, K1 [60 sts].

Row 108: P1, P2tog, P to last 3 sts, P2togtbl, P1 [58 sts].

Row 109: K1, ssK, K to last 3 sts, K2tog, K1 [56 sts].

Row 110: P1, P2tog, P to last 3 sts, P2togtbl, P1 [54 sts].

Row 111: K1, ssK, K to last 3 sts, K2tog, K1 [52 sts].

Row 112: Purl.

Row 113: K1, ssK, K to last 3 sts, K2tog, K1 [50 sts].

Row 114: Purl.

Row 115: K1, ssK, K to last 3 sts, K2tog, K1 [48 sts].

Row 116: Purl.

Row 117: K1, ssK, K to last 3 sts, K2tog, K1 [46 sts].

Row 118: Purl.

Row 119: K1, ssK, K to last 3 sts, K2tog, K1 [44 sts].

Row 120: Purl.

Row 121: K1, ssK, K to last 3 sts, K2tog, K1 [42 sts].

Row 122: Purl.

Row 123: Knit.

Row 124: Purl.

Row 125: K1, ssK, K to last 3 sts, K2tog, K1 [40 sts].

Row 126: Purl.

Row 127: Knit.

Row 128: P1, P2tog, P to last 3 sts, P2togtbl, P1 [38 sts].

Row 129: Knit.

Row 130: Purl.

Row 131: K1, ssK, K to last 3 sts, K2tog, K1 [36 sts].

Row 132: Purl.

Row 133: K1, ssK, K to last 3 sts, K2tog, K1 [34 sts].

Row 134: Purl.

Row 135: K1, ssK, K to last 3 sts, K2tog, K1 [32 sts].

Row 136: Purl.

Row 137: K1, ssK, K to last 3 sts, K2tog, K1 [30 sts].

Row 138: Purl.

Row 139: K1, ssK, K to last 3 sts, K2tog, K1 [28 sts].

Row 140: Purl.

Row 141: K1, ssK, K to last 3 sts, K2tog, K1 [26 sts].

Row 142: Purl.

Row 143: Knit.

Row 144: Purl.

Row 145: Cast off 3 sts at beg of row [23 sts].

Row 146: Cast off 3 sts at beg of row [20 sts].

Row 147: Cast off 4 sts at beg of row [16 sts].

Row 148: Cast off 4 sts at beg of row [12 sts].

Row 149: Cast off rem 12 sts.

Making up

1. Join the right shoulder seam.

2. With RS facing and using 4.5mm (UK 7, US 7) needles, pick up and knit 19 sts along left front edge of neck shaping, knit across 14 sts on st holder and pick up and knit 19 sts along right front neck edge. Pick up and knit 20 sts to centre of back of neck and a further 20 sts to left back shoulder [92 sts].

3. Work 10 rows in (K2, P2) rib and cast off loosely and evenly in rib.

4. Join the left shoulder seam.

5. Lightly press or block all pieces of the sweater and sew the sleeves into the armholes, easing to fit.

6. Follow the finishing instructions for your chosen design, working any embroidery and details.

7. Sew the side seams and underarm seams, being careful to match any pattern.

8. Sew in all loose ends of yarn.

Child: Age 5–6

Front

Using 4.5mm (UK 7, US 7) needles, cast on 64 sts.

Next row: (K2, P2), rep to end of row.

Rep this row a further 7 times.

Working from the Front Chart for your chosen motif, cont as follows:

Work in SS for 56 rows or until work measures 24cm (9½in).

Cont in SS, working decreases as shown to shape armholes:

Row 57: Cast off 3 sts at beg of row [61 sts].

Row 58: Cast off 3 sts at beg of row [58 sts].

Row 59: K1, ssK, K to last 3 sts, K2tog, K1 [56 sts].

Row 60: P1, P2tog, P to last 3 sts, P2togtbl, P1 [54 sts].

Row 61: Knit.

Row 62: P1, P2tog, P to last 3 sts, P2togtbl, P1 [52 sts].

Row 63: Knit.

Row 64: Purl.

Row 65: K1, ssK, K to last 3 sts, K2tog, K1 [50 sts].

Row 66: Purl.

Row 67: Knit.

Row 68: Purl.

Row 69: K1, ssK, K to last 3 sts, K2tog, K1 [48 sts].

Cont with no further shaping until row 78 is complete.

Shape Front Neck as follows:

Row 79: K20, turn, leaving rem sts on a st holder. Cont working over these 20 sts.

Row 80: Cast off 2 sts at beg of row [18 sts].

Row 81: K to last 3 sts, K2tog, K1 [17 sts].

Row 82: P1, P2tog, P to end of row [16 sts].

Row 83: K to last 3 sts, K2tog, K1 [15 sts].

Row 84: Purl.

Row 85: K to last 3 sts, K2tog, K1 [14 sts].

Row 86: Purl.

Row 87: K to last 3 sts, K2tog, K1 [13 sts].

Row 88: Purl.

Row 89: K to last 3 sts, K2tog, K1 [12 sts].

Row 90: Purl.

Row 91: Knit.

Row 92: Purl.

Row 93: Cast off 6 sts at beg of row [6 sts].

Row 94: Purl.

Row 95: Cast off rem 6 sts.

Place centre 8 sts on a st holder and, with RS facing, rejoin yarn to rem 20 sts.

Work second side as follows:

Row 80: Purl.

Row 81: Cast off 2 sts at beg of row [18 sts].

Row 82: P to last 3 sts, P2togtbl, P1 [17 sts].

Row 83: K1, ssK, K to end of row [16 sts].

Row 84: P to last 3 sts, P2togtbl, P1 [15 sts].

Row 85: Knit.

Row 86: P to last 3 sts, P2togtbl, P1 [14 sts].

Row 87: Knit.

Row 88: P to last 3 sts, P2togtbl, P1 [13 sts].

Row 89: Knit.

Row 90: P to last 3 sts, P2togtbl, P1 [12 sts].

Row 91: Knit.

Row 92: Purl.

Row 93: Knit.

Row 94: Cast off 6 sts at beg of row [6 sts].

Row 95: Knit.

Row 96: Cast off rem 6 sts.

Back

Using 4.5mm (UK 7, US 7) needles, cast on 64 sts and work as for Front. Use the Back Chart for your chosen motif and follow the instructions for the Front armhole shaping up to end of row 69 [48 sts].

With no further shaping, cont in SS until row 90 is complete.

Row 91: K15, cast off 18 sts and K to end of row. Cont over rem 15 sts, setting aside the other set of 15 sts to be completed later.

Row 92: P to last 3 sts, P2togtbl, P1 [14 sts].

Row 93: K1, ssK, K to end of row [13 sts].

Row 94: Cast off 6 sts, P to last 3 sts, P2togtbl, P1 [6 sts].

Row 95: Knit.

Row 96: Cast off rem 6 sts.

With WS facing, rejoin yarn to rem 15 sts and cont as follows:

Row 92: P1, P2tog, P to end of row [14 sts].

Row 93: Cast off 6 sts, K to last 3 sts, K2tog, K1 [7 sts].

Row 94: P1, P2tog, P to end of row [6 sts].

Row 95: Cast off rem 6 sts.

Sleeves (make two)

Using 4.5mm (UK 7, US 7) needles, cast on 36 sts and work 8 rows in (K2, P2) rib, as for Front.

Cont in SS for 53 rows, working from Sleeve Chart if appropriate, and shaping as follows:

Inc 1 st at each end of rows 6, 15, 25, 35, 44 and 53 as follows: K1, M1, K to last st, M1, K1.

At the end of row 53 there will be 48 sts on the needle.

Cont in SS with no further shaping until row 62 is complete or until sleeve measures 26.5cm (10½in).

Work sleeve-head shaping as follows:

Row 63: Cast off 3 sts at beg of row [45 sts].

Row 64: Cast off 3 sts at beg of row [42 sts].

Row 65: Cast off 3 sts at beg of row [39 sts].

Row 66: Cast off 3 sts at beg of row [36 sts].

Row 67: K1, ssK, K to last 3 sts, K2tog, K1 [34 sts].

Row 68: P1, P2tog, P to last 3 sts, P2togtbl, P1 [32 sts].

Row 69: Knit.

Row 70: P1, P2tog, P to last 3 sts, P2togtbl, P1 [30 sts].

Row 71: Knit.

Row 72: P1, P2tog, P to last 3 sts, P2togtbl, P1 [28 sts].

Row 73: Knit.

Row 74: Purl.

Row 75: K1, ssK, K to last 3 sts, K2tog, K1 [26 sts].

Row 76: Purl.

Row 77: K1, ssK, K to last 3 sts, K2tog, K1 [24 sts].

Row 78: Purl.

Row 79: Knit.

Row 80: P1, P2tog, P to last 3 sts, P2togtbl, P1 [22 sts].

Row 81: Knit.

Row 82: Purl.

Row 83: K1, ssK, K to last 3 sts, K2tog, K1 [20 sts].

Row 84: Purl.

Row 85: K1, ssK, K to last 3 sts, K2tog, K1 [18 sts].

Row 86: Purl.

Row 87: K1, ssK, K to last 3 sts, K2tog, K1 [16 sts].

Row 88: Cast off 3 sts at beg of row [13 sts].

Row 89: Cast off 3 sts at beg of row [10 sts].

Row 90: Purl.

Row 91: Cast off rem 10 sts.

Making up

1. Join the right shoulder seam.

2. With RS facing and using 4.5mm (UK 7, US 7) needles, pick up and knit 15 sts along left front edge of neck shaping, knit across 8 sts on st holder and pick up and knit 15 sts along right front neck edge. Pick up and knit 13 sts to centre of back of neck and a further 13 sts to left back shoulder [64 sts].

3. Work 6 rows in (K2, P2) rib and cast off loosely and evenly in rib.

4. Join the left shoulder seam.

5. Lightly press or block all pieces of the sweater and sew the sleeves into the armholes, easing to fit.

6. Follow the finishing instructions for your chosen design, working any embroidery and details.

7. Sew the side seams and underarm seams, being careful to match any pattern.

8. Sew in all loose ends of yarn.

Child: Age 7–8

Front

Using 4.5mm (UK 7, US 7) needles, cast on 70 sts.

Row 1: (K2, P2) to last 2 sts, K2.

Row 2: (P2, K2) to last 2 sts, P2.

Rep rows 1 and 2 three more times.

Working from the Front Chart for your chosen motif, cont as follows:

Work in SS for 66 rows or until work measures 28cm (11in).

Cont in SS, working decreases as shown to shape armholes:

Row 67: Cast off 5 sts at beg of row [65 sts].

Row 68: Cast off 5 sts at beg of row [60 sts].

Row 69: K1, ssK, K to last 3 sts, K2tog, K1 [58 sts].

Row 70: P1, P2tog, P to last 3 sts, P2togtbl, P1 [56 sts].

Row 71: Knit.

Row 72: P1, P2tog, P to last 3 sts, P2togtbl, P1 [54 sts].

Row 73: Knit.

Row 74: Purl.

Row 75: K1, ssK, K to last 3 sts, K2tog, K1 [52 sts].

Row 76: Purl.

Row 77: Knit.

Row 78: Purl.

Row 79: Knit.

Row 80: P1, P2tog, P to last 3 sts, P2togtbl, P1 [50 sts].

Cont with no further shaping until row 94 is complete.

Shape Front Neck as follows:

Row 95: K19, turn, leaving rem sts on a st holder. Cont working over these 19 sts.

Row 96: P1, P2tog, P to end of row [18 sts].

Row 97: K to last 3 sts, K2tog, K1 [17 sts].

Row 98: P1, P2tog, P to end of row [16 sts].

Row 99: Knit.

Row 100: P1, P2tog, P to end of row [15 sts].

Row 101: K to last 3 sts, K2tog, K1 [14 sts].

Row 102: Purl.

Row 103: K to last 3 sts, K2tog, K1 [13 sts].

Row 104: Purl.

Row 105: Knit.

Row 106: P1, P2tog, P to end of row [12 sts].

Row 107: Knit.

Row 108: Purl.

Row 109: Cast off 6 sts at beg of row [6 sts].

Row 110: Purl.

Row 111: Cast off rem 6 sts.

Place centre 12 sts on a holder and, with RS facing, rejoin yarn to rem 19 st. K to end of row.

Work second side as follows:

Row 96: P to last 3 sts, P2togtbl, P1 [18 sts].

Row 97: K1, ssK, K to end of row [17 sts].

Row 98: P to last 3 sts, P2togtbl, P1 [16 sts].

Row 99: Knit.

Row 100: P to last 3 sts, P2togtbl, P1 [15 sts].

Row 101: K1, ssK, K to end of row [14 sts].

Row 102: Purl.

Row 103: K1, ssK, K to end of row [13 sts].

Row 104: Purl.

Row 105: Knit.

Row 106: P to last 3 sts, P2togtbl, P1 [12 sts].

Row 107: Knit.

Row 108: Purl.

Row 109: Knit.

Row 110: Cast off 6 sts at beg of row [6 sts].

Row 111: Knit.

Row 112: Cast off rem 6 sts.

Back

Using 4.5mm (UK 7, US 7) needles, cast on 70 sts and work as for Front. Use the Back Chart for your chosen motif and follow the instructions for the Front armhole shaping up to end of row 80 [50 sts].

With no further shaping, cont in SS until row 102 is complete.

Row 103: K16, cast off 18 sts and K to end of row. Cont over rem 16 sts, setting aside the other set of 16 sts to be completed later.

Row 104: Purl.

Row 105: Cast off 2 sts at beg of row [14 sts].

Row 106: P to last 3 sts, P2togtbl, P1 [13 sts].

Row 107: K1, ssK, K to end of row [12 sts].

Row 108: Purl.

Row 109: Knit.

Row 110: Cast off 6 sts at beg of row [6 sts].

Row 111: Knit.

Row 112: Cast off rem 6 sts.

With WS facing, rejoin yarn to rem 16 sts and cont as follows:

Row 104: Cast off 2 sts at beg of row [14 sts].

Row 105: K to last 3 sts, K2tog, K1 [13 sts].

Row 106: P1, P2tog, P to end of row [12 sts].

Row 107: Knit.

Row 108: Purl.

Row 109: Cast off 6 sts at beg of row [6 sts].

Row 110: Purl.

Row 111: Cast off rem 6 sts.

Sleeves (make two)

Using 4.5mm (UK 7, US 7) needles, cast on 38 sts and work 8 rows in (K2, P2) rib, as for Front.

Cont in SS for 64 rows, working from Sleeve Chart if appropriate, and shaping as follows:

Inc 1 st at each end of rows 6, 16, 25, 35, 45, 54 and 64 as follows: K1, M1, K to last st, M1, K1.

At the end of row 64 there will be 52 sts on the needle.

Cont in SS with no further shaping until row 68 is complete or until sleeve measures 29cm (11½in).

Work sleeve-head shaping as follows:

Row 69: Cast off 3 sts at beg of row [49 sts].

Row 70: Cast off 3 sts at beg of row [46 sts].

Row 71: Cast off 3 sts at beg of row [43 sts].

Row 72: Cast off 3 sts at beg of row [40 sts].

Row 73: K1, ssK, K to last 3 sts, K2tog, K1 [38 sts].

Row 74: P1, P2tog, P to last 3 sts, P2togtbl, P1 [36 sts].

Row 75: Knit.

Row 76: P1, P2tog, P to last 3 sts, P2togtbl, P1 [34 sts].

Row 77: Knit.

Row 78: P1, P2tog, P to last 3 sts, P2togtbl, P1 [32 sts].

Row 79: Knit.

Row 80: P1, P2tog, P to last 3 sts, P2togtbl, P1 [30 sts].

Row 81: Knit.

Row 82: Purl.

Row 83: K1, ssK, K to last 3 sts, K2tog, K1 [28 sts].

Row 84: Purl.

Row 85: K1, ssK, K to last 3 sts, K2tog, K1 [26 sts].

Row 86: Purl.

Row 87: Knit.

Row 88: P1, P2tog, P to last 3 sts, P2togtbl, P1 [24 sts].

Row 89: Knit.

Row 90: Purl.

Row 91: K1, ssK, K to last 3 sts, K2tog, K1 [22 sts].

Row 92: Purl.

Row 93: K1, ssK, K to last 3 sts, K2tog, K1 [20 sts].

Row 94: Purl.

Row 95: K1, ssK, K to last 3 sts, K2tog, K1 [18 sts].

Row 96: Purl.

Row 97: K1, ssK, K to last 3 sts, K2tog, K1 [16 sts].

Row 98: Purl.

Row 99: Cast off 3 sts at beg of row [13 sts].

Row 100: Cast off 3 sts at beg of row [10 sts].

Row 101: Cast off rem 10 sts.

Making up

1. Join the right shoulder seam.

2. With RS facing and using 4.5mm (UK 7, US 7) needles, pick up and knit 14 sts along left front edge of neck shaping, knit across 12 sts on st holder and pick up and knit 14 sts along right front neck edge. Pick up and knit 18 sts to centre of back of neck and a further 18 sts to left back shoulder [76 sts].

3. Work 6 rows in (K2, P2) rib and cast off loosely and evenly in rib.

4. Join the left shoulder seam.

5. Lightly press or block all pieces of the sweater and sew the sleeves into the armholes, easing to fit.

6. Follow the finishing instructions for your chosen design, working any embroidery and details.

7. Sew the side seams and underarm seams, being careful to match any pattern.

8. Sew in all loose ends of yarn.

Child: Age 9–10

Front

Using 4.5mm (UK 7, US 7) needles, cast on 74 sts.

Row 1: (K2, P2) to last 2 sts, K2.

Row 2: (P2, K2) to last 2 sts, P2.

Rep rows 1 and 2 three more times.

Working from the Front Chart for your chosen motif, cont as follows:

Work in SS for 74 rows or until work measures 30cm (11¾in).

Cont in SS, working decreases as shown to shape armholes:

Row 75: Cast off 4 sts at beg of row [70 sts].

Row 76: Cast off 4 sts at beg of row [66 sts].

Row 77: K1, ssK, K to last 3 sts, K2tog, K1 [64 sts].

Row 78: P1, P2tog, P to last 3 sts, P2tog, P1 [62 sts].

Row 79: K1, ssK, K to last 3 sts, K2tog, K1 [60 sts].

Row 80: Purl.

Row 81: K1, ssK, K to last 3 sts, K2tog, K1 [58 sts].

Row 82: Purl.

Row 83: Knit.

Row 84: P1, P2tog, P to last 3 sts, P2tog, P1 [56 sts].

Row 85: Knit.

Row 86: Purl.

Row 87: Knit.

Row 88: Purl.

Row 89: K1, ssK, K to last 3 sts, K2tog, K1 [54 sts].

Cont with no further shaping until row 104 is complete.

Shape Front Neck as follows:

Row 105: K21, turn, leaving rem sts on a st holder. Cont working over these 21 sts.

Row 106: P1, P2tog, P to end of row [20 sts].

Row 107: K to last 3 sts, K2tog, K1 [19 sts].

Row 108: P1, P2tog, P to end of row [18 sts].

Row 109: K to last 3 sts, K2tog, K1 [17 sts].

Row 110: Purl.

Row 111: K to last 3 sts, K2tog, K1 [16 sts].

Row 112: Purl.

Row 113: K to last 3 sts, K2tog, K1 [15 sts].

Row 114: Purl.

Row 115: K to last 3 sts, K2tog, K1 [14 sts].

Row 116: Purl.

Row 117: Knit.

Row 118: Purl.

Row 119: Cast off 6 sts at beg of row, K to last 3 sts, K2tog, K1 [7 sts].

Row 120: Purl.

Row 121: Cast off rem 7 sts.

Place centre 12 sts on a st holder and, with RS facing, rejoin yarn to rem 21 sts. K to end of row.

Work second side as follows:

Row 106: P to last 3 sts, P2togtbl, P1 [20 sts].

Row 107: K1, ssK, K to end of row [19 sts].

Row 108: P to last 3 sts, P2togtbl, P1 [18 sts].

Row 109: K1, ssK, K to end of row [17 sts].

Row 110: Purl.

Row 111: K1, ssK, K to end of row [16 sts].

Row 112: Purl.

Row 113: K1, ssK, K to end of row [15 sts].

Row 114: Purl.

Row 115: K1, ssK, K to end of row [14 sts].

Row 116: Purl.

Row 117: Knit.

Row 118: Purl.

Row 119: Knit.

Row 120: Cast off 6 sts at beg of row, P to last 3 sts, P2togtbl, P1 [7 sts].

Row 121: Knit.

Row 122: Cast off rem 7 sts.

Back

Using 4.5mm (UK 7, US 7) needles, cast on 74 sts and work as for Front. Use the Back Chart for your chosen motif and follow the instructions for armhole shaping up to end of row 89 [54 sts]. With no further shaping, cont in SS until row 114 is complete.

Row 115: K18, cast off 18 sts and K to end of row. Cont over rem 18 sts, setting aside the other set of 18 sts to be completed later.

Row 116: Purl.

Row 117: Cast off 3 sts at beg of row [15 sts].

Row 118: Purl.

Row 119: K1, ssK, K to end of row [14 sts].

Row 120: Cast off 6 sts at beg of row [8 sts].

Row 121: K1, ssK, K to end of row [7 sts].

Row 122: Cast off rem 7 sts.

With WS facing, rejoin yarn to rem 18 sts and cont as follows:

Row 116: Cast off 3 sts at beg of row [15 sts].

Row 117: Knit.

Row 118: P1, P2tog, P to end of row [14 sts].

Row 119: Cast off 6 sts at beg of row [8 sts].

Row 120: P1, P2tog, P to end of row [7 sts].

Row 121: Cast off rem 7 sts.

Sleeves (make two)

Using 4.5mm (UK 7, US 7) needles, cast on 40 sts and work 8 rows in (K2, P2) rib.

Cont in SS for 76 rows, working from Sleeve Chart if appropriate, and shaping as follows:

Inc 1 st at each end of rows 12, 21, 30, 39, 49, 58, 67 and 76 as follows: K1, M1, K to last st, M1, K1.

At the end of row 76 there will be 56 sts on the needle.

Cont in SS with no further shaping until row 80 is complete or until sleeve measures 34cm (13½in).

Work sleeve-head shaping as follows:

Row 81: Cast off 4 sts at beg of row [52 sts].

Row 82: Cast off 4 sts at beg of row [48 sts].

Row 83: Cast off 3 sts at beg of row [45 sts].

Row 84: Cast off 3 sts at beg of row [42 sts].

Row 85: K1, ssK, K to last 3 sts, K2tog, K1 [40 sts].

Row 86: P1, P2tog, P to last 3 sts, P2togtbl, P1 [38 sts].

Row 87: K1, ssK, K to last 3 sts, K2tog, K1 [36 sts].

Row 88: Purl.

Row 89: K1, ssK, K to last 3 sts, K2tog, K1 [34 sts].

Row 90: Purl.

Row 91: K1, ssK, K to last 3 sts, K2tog, K1 [32 sts].

Row 92: Purl.

Row 93: Knit.

Row 94: P1, P2tog, P to last 3 sts, P2togtbl, P1 [30 sts].

Row 95: Knit.

Row 96: Purl.

Row 97: K1, ssK, K to last 3 sts, K2tog, K1 [28 sts].

Row 98: Purl.

Row 99: K1, ssK, K to last 3 sts, K2tog, K1 [26 sts].

Row 100: Purl.

Row 101: Knit.

Row 102: Purl.

Row 103: K1, ssK, K to last 3 sts, K2tog, K1 [24 sts].

Row 104: Purl.

Row 105: K1, ssK, K to last 3 sts, K2tog, K1 [22 sts].

Row 106: Purl.

Row 107: K1, ssK, K to last 3 sts, K2tog, K1 [20 sts].

Row 108: Purl.

Row 109: K1, ssK, K to last 3 sts, K2tog, K1 [18 sts].

Row 110: P1, P2tog, P to last 3 sts, P2togtbl, P1 [16 sts].

Row 111: K1, ssK, K to last 3 sts, K2tog, K1 [14 sts].

Row 112: P1, P2tog, P to last 3 sts, P2togtbl, P1 [12 sts].

Row 113: Cast off rem 12 sts.

Making up

1. Join the right shoulder seam.

2. With RS facing and using 4.5mm (UK 7, US 7) needles, pick up and knit 14 sts along left front edge of neck shaping, knit across 12 sts on st holder and pick up and knit 14 sts along right front neck edge. Pick up and knit 20 sts to centre of back of neck and a further 20 sts to left back shoulder [80 sts].

3. Work 6 rows in (K2, P2) rib and cast off loosely and evenly in rib.

4. Join the left shoulder seam.

5. Lightly press or block all pieces of the sweater and sew the sleeves into the armholes, easing to fit.

6. Follow the finishing instructions for your chosen design, working any embroidery and details.

7. Sew the side seams and underarm seams, being careful to match any pattern.

8. Sew in all loose ends of yarn.

Child: Age 11–12

Front

Using 4.5mm (UK 7, US 7) needles, cast on 78 sts.

Row 1: (K2, P2) to last 2 sts, P2.

Row 2: (P2, K2) to last 2 sts, K2.

Rep rows 1 and 2 three more times.

Working from the Front Chart for your chosen motif, cont as follows:

Work in SS for 76 rows or until work measures 33cm (13in).

Cont in SS, working decreases as shown to shape armholes:

Row 77: Cast off 5 sts at beg of row [73 sts].

Row 78: Cast off 5 sts at beg of row [68 sts].

Row 79: K1, ssK, K to last 3 sts, K2tog, K1 [66 sts].

Row 80: P1, P2tog, P to last 3 sts, P2togtbl, P1 [64 sts].

Row 81: Knit.

Row 82: P1, P2tog, P to last 3 sts, P2togtbl, P1 [62 sts].

Row 83: Knit.

Row 84: P1, P2tog, P to last 3 sts, P2togtbl, P1 [60 sts].

Row 85: Knit.

Row 86: Purl.

Row 87: K1, ssK, K to last 3 sts, K2tog, K1 [58 sts].

Row 88: Purl.

Row 89: Knit.

Row 90: Purl.

Row 91: Knit.

Row 92: Purl.

Row 93: K1, ssK, K to last 3 sts, K2tog, K1 [56 sts].

Cont with no further shaping until row 106 is complete.

Shape Front Neck as follows:

Row 107: K25, turn, leaving rem sts on a st holder. Cont working over these 25 sts.

Row 108: Cast off 4 sts at beg of row [21 sts].

Row 109: Knit.

Row 110: P1, P2tog, P to end of row [20 sts].

Row 111: K to last 3 sts, K2tog, K1 [19 sts].

Row 112: P1, P2tog, P to end of row [18 sts].

Row 113: K to last 3 sts, K2tog, K1 [17 sts].

Row 114: Purl.

Row 115: K to last 3 sts, K2tog, K1 [16 sts].

Row 116: Purl.

Row 117: Knit.

Row 118: P1, P2tog, P to end of row [15 sts].

Row 119: Knit.

Row 120: P1, P2tog, P to end of row [14 sts].

Row 121: Knit.

Row 122: P1, P2tog, P to end of row [13 sts].

Row 123: Cast off 7 sts at beg of row [6 sts].

Row 124: Purl.

Row 125: Cast off rem 6 sts.

Place centre 6 sts on a st holder and, with RS facing, rejoin yarn to rem 25 sts. K to end of row.

Work second side as follows:

Row 108: Purl.

Row 109: Cast off 4 sts at beg of row [21 sts].

Row 110: P to last 3 sts, P2togtbl, P1 [20 sts].

Row 111: K1, ssK, K to end of row [19 sts].

Row 112: P to last 3 sts, P2togtbl, P1 [18 sts].

Row 113: K1, ssK, K to end of row [17 sts].

Row 114: Purl.

Row 115: K1, ssK, K to end of row [16 sts].

Row 116: Purl.

Row 117: Knit.

Row 118: P to last 3 sts, P2togtbl, P1 [15 sts].

Row 119: Knit.

Row 120: P to last 3 sts, P2togtbl, P1 [14 sts].

Row 121: Knit.

Row 122: P to last 3 sts, P2togtbl, P1 [13 sts].

Row 123: Knit.

Row 124: Cast off 7 sts at beg of row [6 sts].

Row 125: Knit.

Row 126: Cast off rem 6 sts.

Back

Using 4.5mm (UK 7, US 7) needles, cast on 78 sts and work as for Front. Use the Back Chart for your chosen motif and follow the instructions for armhole shaping up to end of row 93 [56 sts].

With no further shaping, cont in SS until row 118 is complete.

Row 119: K19, cast off 18 sts and K to end of row. Cont over rem 19 sts, setting aside the other set of 19 sts to be completed later.

Row 120: P to last 3 sts, P2togtbl, P1 [18 sts].

Row 121: Cast off 2 sts at beg of row [16 sts].

Row 122: Purl.

Row 123: K1, ssK, K to end of row [15 sts].

Row 124: Cast off 7 sts at beg of row, P to last 3 sts, P2togtbl, P1 [7 sts].

Row 125: K1, ssK, K to end of row [6 sts].

Row 126: Cast off rem 6 sts.

With WS facing, rejoin yarn to rem 19 sts and cont as follows:

Row 120: Cast off 2 sts at beg of row [17 sts].

Row 121: K to last 3 sts, K2tog, K1 [16 sts].

Row 122: P1, P2tog, P to end of row [15 sts].

Row 123: Cast off 7 sts at beg of row, K to last 3 sts, K2tog, K1 [7 sts].

Row 124: P1, P2tog, P to end of row [6 sts].

Row 125: Cast off rem 6 sts.

Sleeves (make two)

Using 4.5mm (UK 7, US 7) needles, cast on 40 sts and work 8 rows in (K2, P2) rib.

Cont in SS for 83 rows, working from Sleeve Chart if appropriate, and shaping as follows:

Inc 1 st at each end of rows 12, 21, 30, 39, 47, 56, 65, 74 and 83 as follows: K1, M1, K to last st, M1, K1.

At the end of row 83 there will be 58 sts on the needle.

Cont in SS with no further shaping until row 86 is complete or until sleeve measures 36cm (14¼in).

Work sleeve-head shaping as follows:

Row 87: Cast off 6 sts at beg of row [52 sts].

Row 88: Cast off 6 sts at beg of row [46 sts].

Row 89: K1, ssK, K to last 3 sts, K2tog, K1 [44 sts].

Row 90: P1, P2tog, P to last 3 sts, P2togtbl, P1 [42 sts].

Row 91: Knit.

Row 92: P1, P2tog, P to last 3 sts, P2togtbl, P1 [40 sts].

Row 93: K1, ssK, K to last 3 sts, K2tog, K1 [38 sts].

Row 94: Purl.

Row 95: K1, ssK, K to last 3 sts, K2tog, K1 [36 sts].

Row 96: P1, P2tog, P to last 3 sts, P2togtbl, P1 [34 sts].

Row 97: Knit.

Row 98: Purl.

Row 99: K1, ssK, K to last 3 sts, K2tog, K1 [32 sts].

Row 100: Purl.

Row 101: Knit.

Row 102: P1, P2tog, P to last 3 sts, P2togtbl, P1 [30 sts].

Row 103: Knit.

Row 104: Purl.

Row 105: K1, ssK, K to last 3 sts, K2tog, K1 [28 sts].

Row 106: Purl.

Row 107: K1, ssK, K to last 3 sts, K2tog, K1 [26 sts].

Row 108: Purl.

Row 109: Knit.

Row 110: Purl.

Row 111: K1, ssK, K to last 3 sts, K2tog, K1 [24 sts].

Row 112: Purl.

Row 113: K1, ssK, K to last 3 sts, K2tog, K1 [22 sts].

Row 114: Purl.

Row 115: K1, ssK, K to last 3 sts, K2tog, K1 [20 sts].

Row 116: Purl.

Row 117: K1, ssK, K to last 3 sts, K2tog, K1 [18 sts].

Row 118: Purl.

Row 119: Cast off 2 sts at beg of row [16 sts].

Row 120: Cast off 2 sts at beg of row [14 sts].

Row 121: Cast off rem 14 sts.

Making up

1. Join the right shoulder seam.

2. With RS facing and using 4.5mm (UK 7, US 7) needles, pick up and knit 20 sts along left front edge of neck shaping, knit across 6 sts on holder and pick up and knit 20 sts along right front neck edge. Pick up and knit 16 sts to centre of back of neck and a further 16 sts to left back shoulder [78 sts].

3. Work 6 rows in (K2, P2) rib and cast off loosely and evenly in rib.

4. Join the left shoulder seam.

5. Lightly press or block all pieces of the sweater and sew the sleeves into the armholes, easing to fit.

6. Follow the finishing instructions for your chosen design, working any embroidery and details.

7. Sew the side seams and underarm seams, being careful to match any pattern.

8. Sew in all loose ends of yarn.

The motifs

There are six sweater designs altogether, with an adult and a child version of each one, all of which are shown in the images below and opposite. Once you have decided which one to knit, go to the appropriate page (the page numbers are provided underneath the photographs) where you will find more information on the designs and motifs themselves;

Adult sweaters

Snowman, page 34

Winter Trees, page 39

Nordic Fair Isle, page 42

Christmas Pudding, page 45

Reindeer, page 54

Santa Claus, page 59

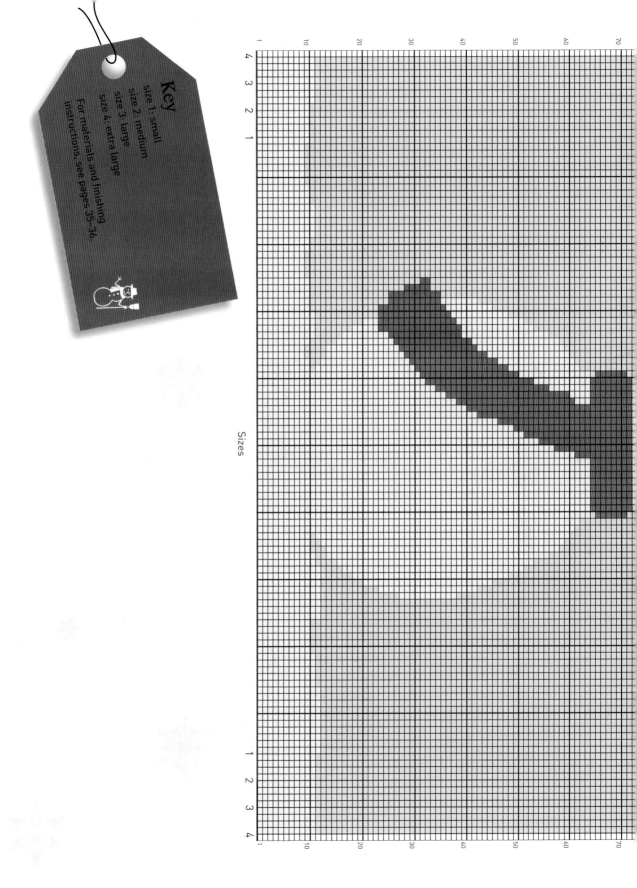

Sizes

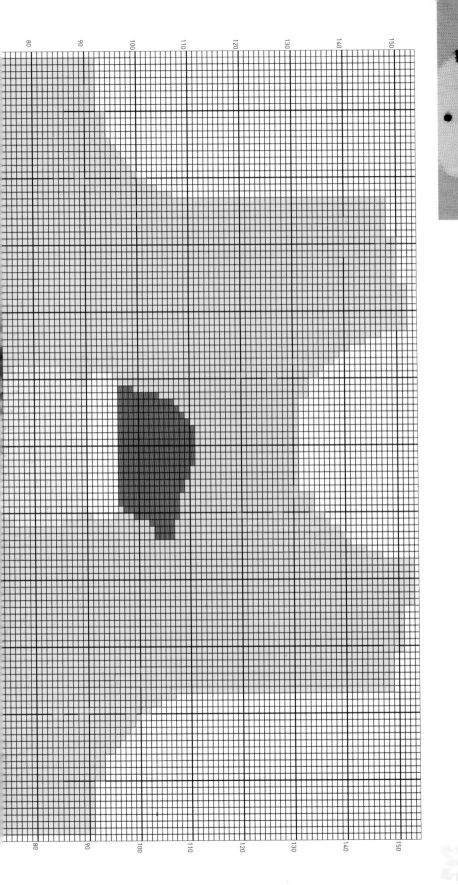

1 Snowman:
ADULT FRONT

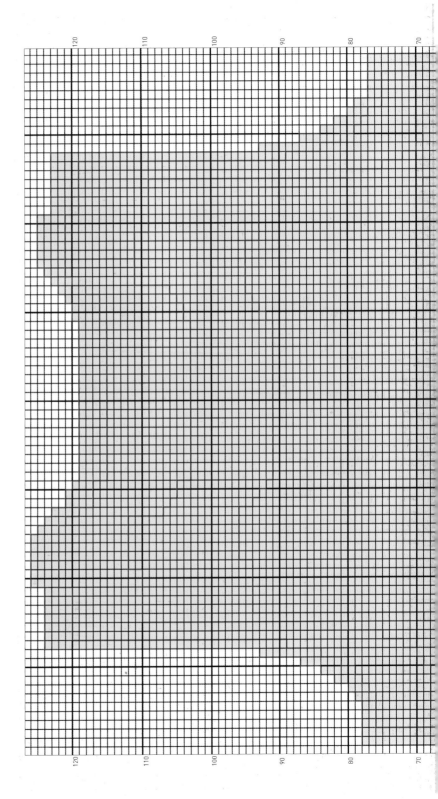

4 Snowman: CHILD BACK

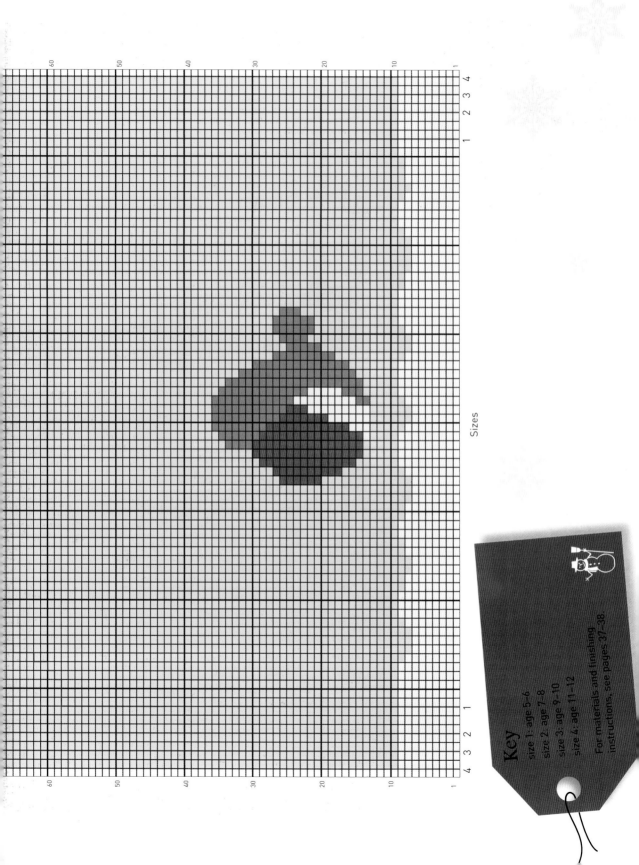

Sizes

Key

size 1: age 5–6
size 2: age 7–8
size 3: age 9–10
size 4: age 11–12

For materials and finishing
instructions, see pages 37–38.

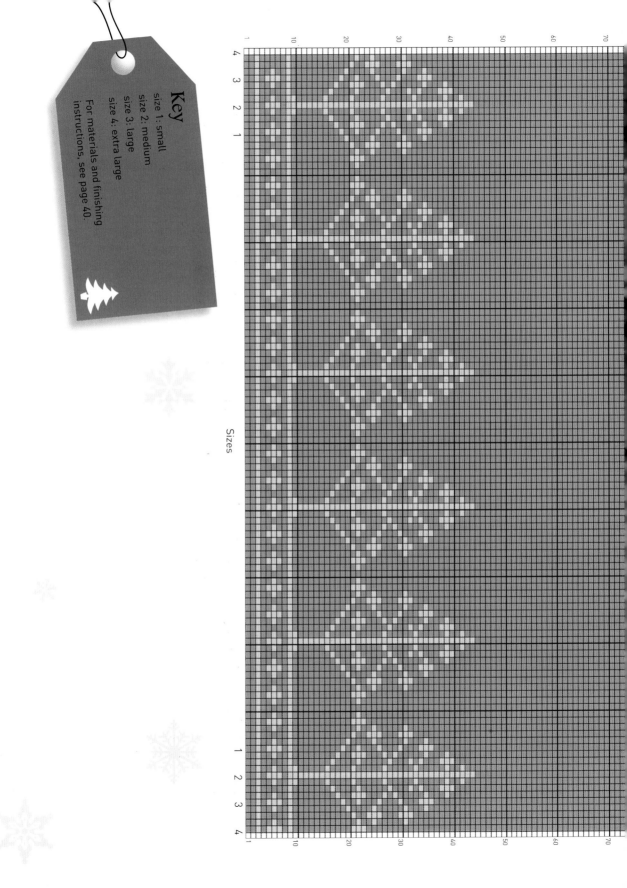

Sizes

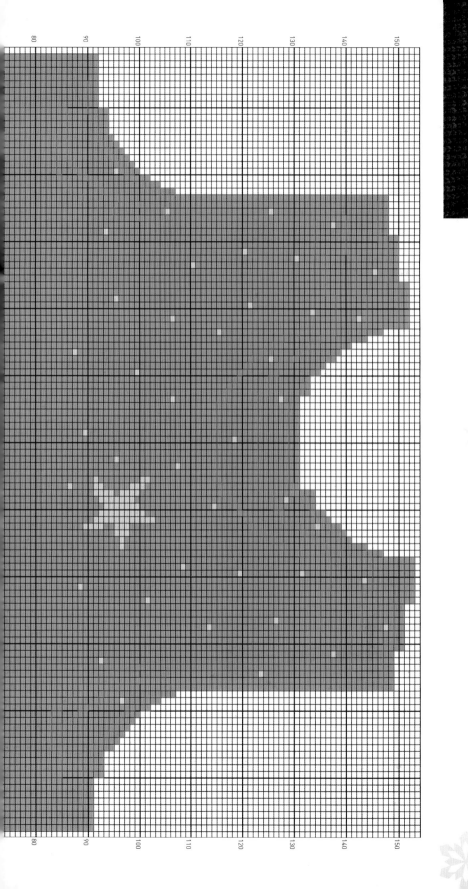

5 Winter Trees:
ADULT FRONT

8 Winter Trees: CHILD FRONT

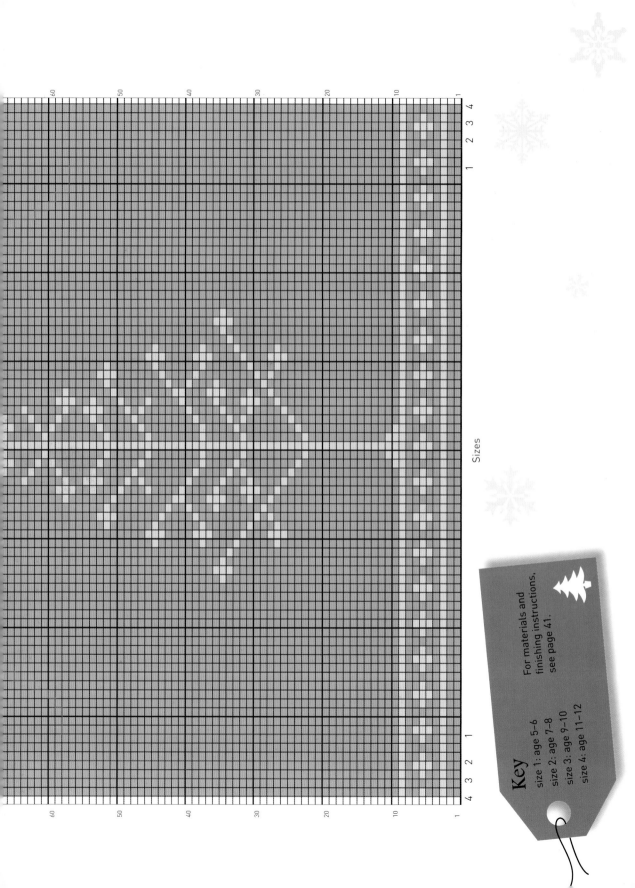

Sizes

Key

size 1: age 5–6
size 2: age 7–8
size 3: age 9–10
size 4: age 11–12

For materials and
finishing instructions.
see page 41.

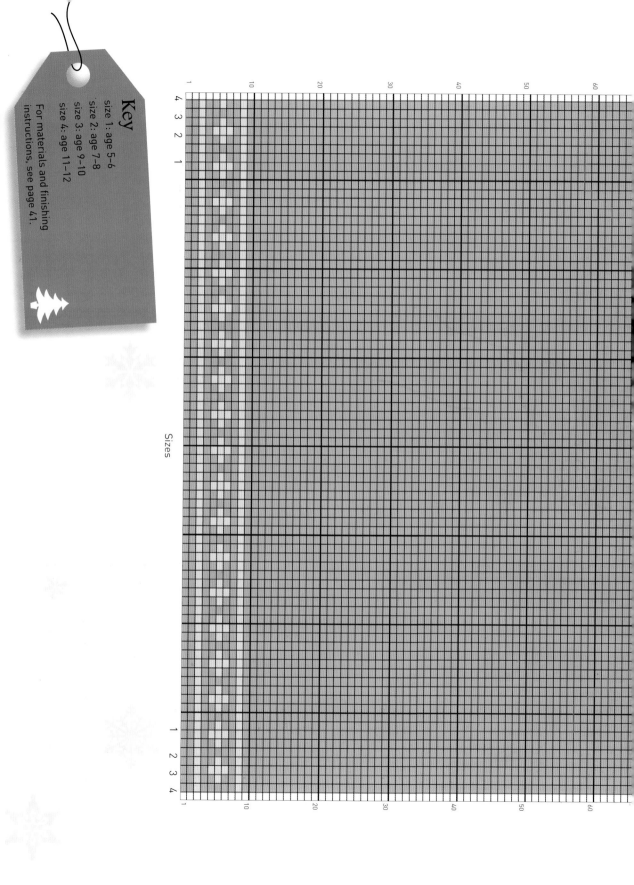

For materials and finishing
instructions, see page 41.

Key

size 1: age 5-6
size 2: age 7-8
size 3: age 9-10
size 4: age 11-12

Sizes

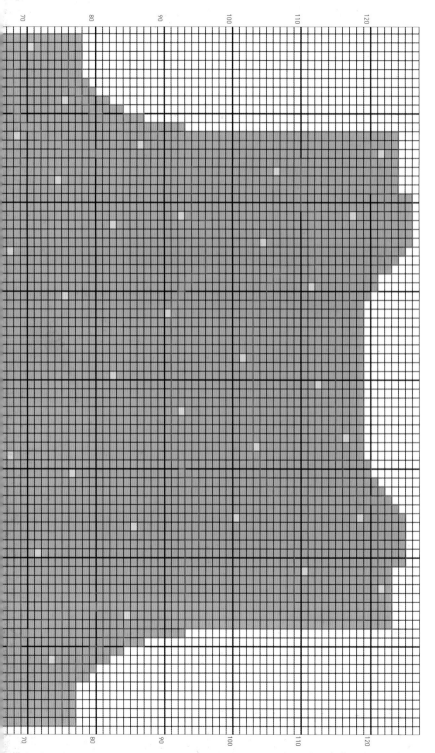

9 Winter Trees: CHILD BACK

12 Nordic Fair Isle: ADULT BACK

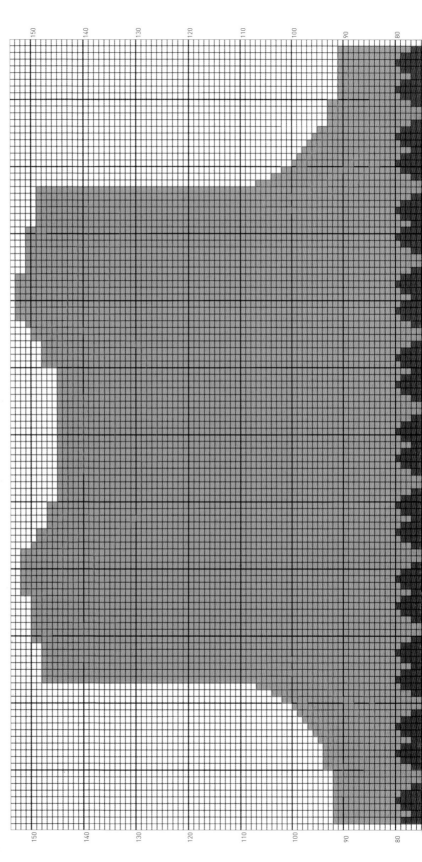

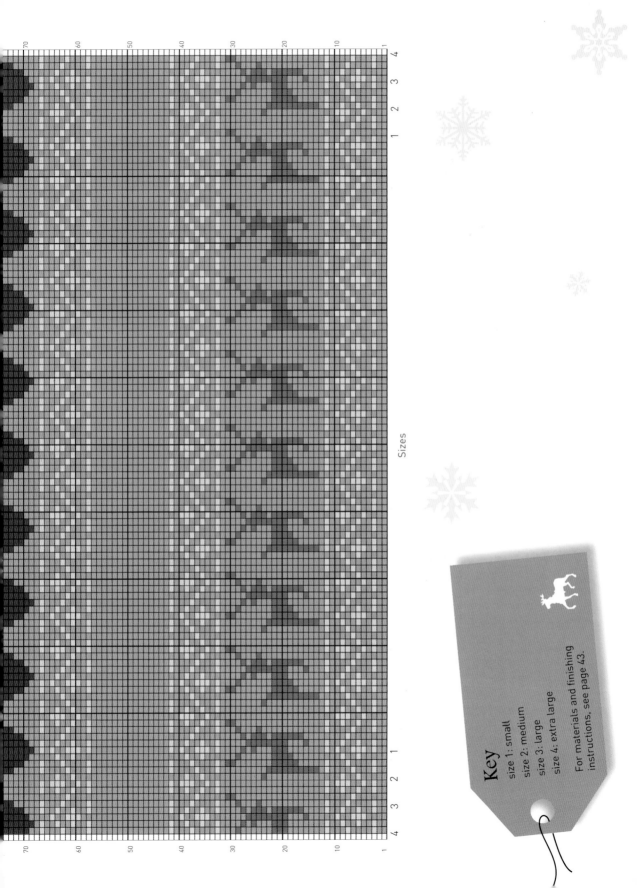

Sizes

Key

size 1: small
size 2: medium
size 3: large
size 4: extra large

For materials and finishing
instructions, see page 43.

Key

size 1: small
size 2: medium
size 3: large
size 4: extra large

For materials and
finishing instructions,
see page 43.

Sizes

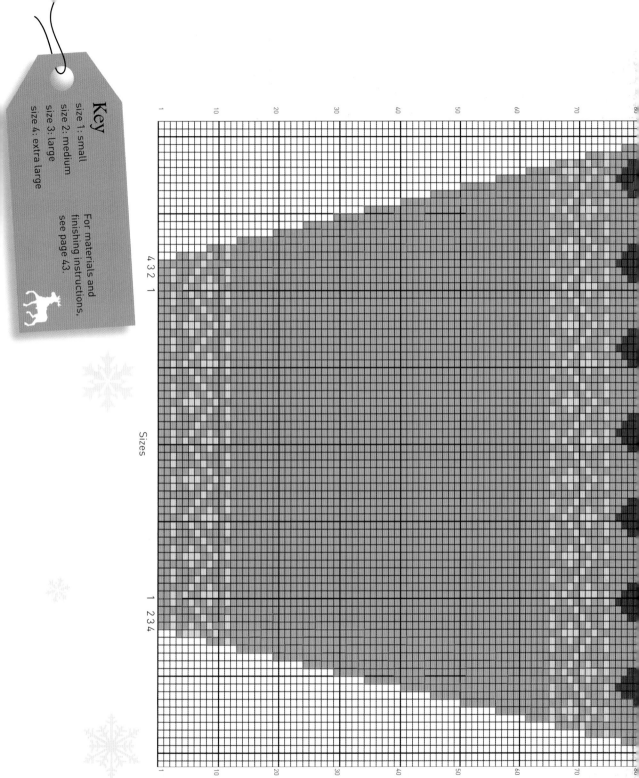

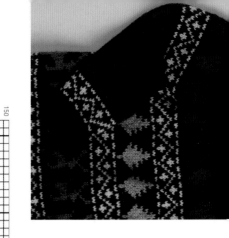

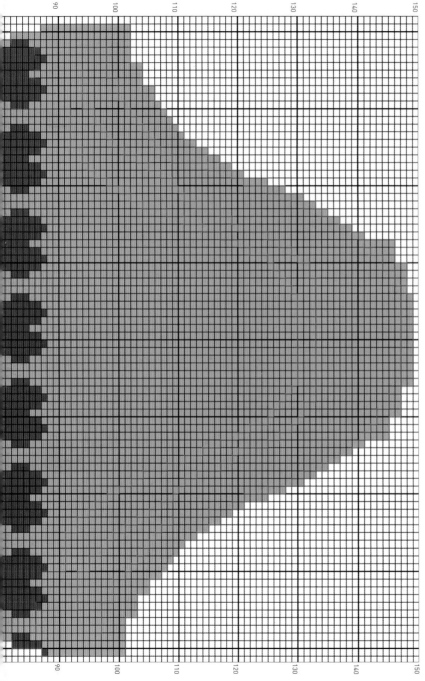

13 Nordic Fair Isle: ADULT SLEEVE

16 Nordic Fair Isle: CHILD SLEEVE

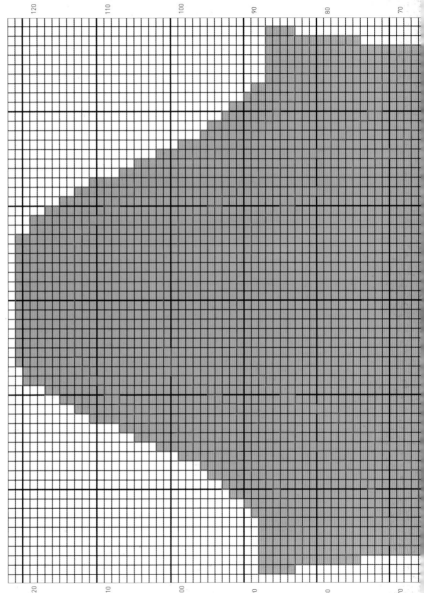

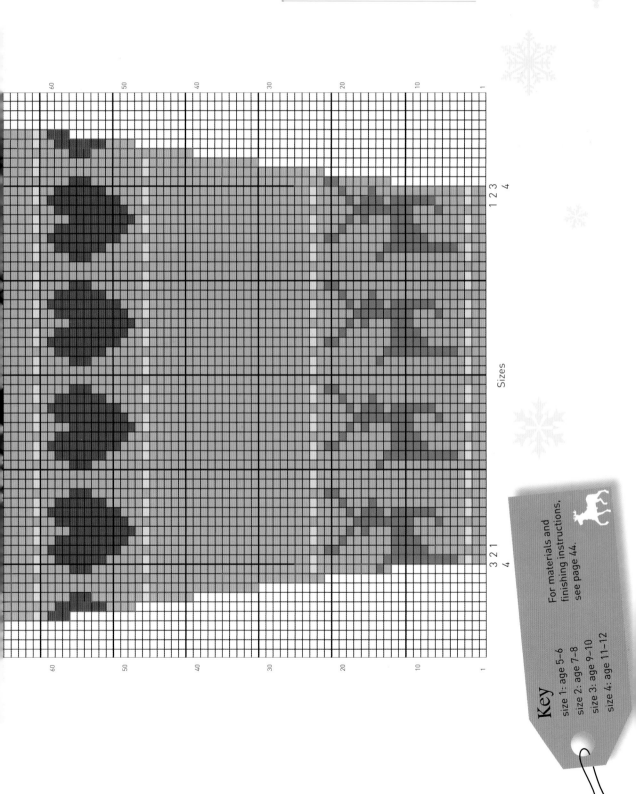

Sizes

1 2 3
4

3 2 1
4

Key

size 1: age 5–6
size 2: age 7–8
size 3: age 9–10
size 4: age 11–12

For materials and
finishing instructions,
see page 44.

Child Front and Back

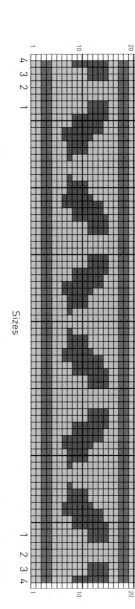

Sizes

Child Sleeve

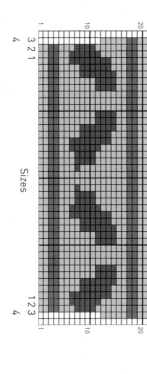

Sizes

Key

size 1: adult small; child age 5–6
size 2: adult medium; child age 7–8
size 3: adult large; child age 9–10
size 4: adult extra large; child age 11–12

For materials and finishing
instructions, see pages 46–52.

17 Christmas Pudding:
ADULT & CHILD
FRONT, BACK & SLEEVE

Note

Follow the relevant chart for 20 rows, then continue in stocking stitch. The Christmas Pudding motif is knitted separately and then sewn on to the Front of the sweater. The patterns for the adult and the child versions of the pudding are provided on pages 46–52.

Adult Front and Back

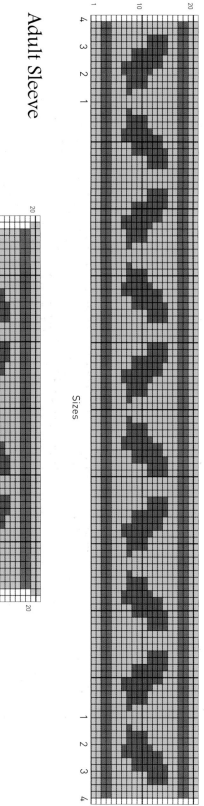

Sizes

Adult Sleeve

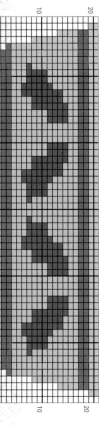

20 Reindeer: ADULT SLEEVE

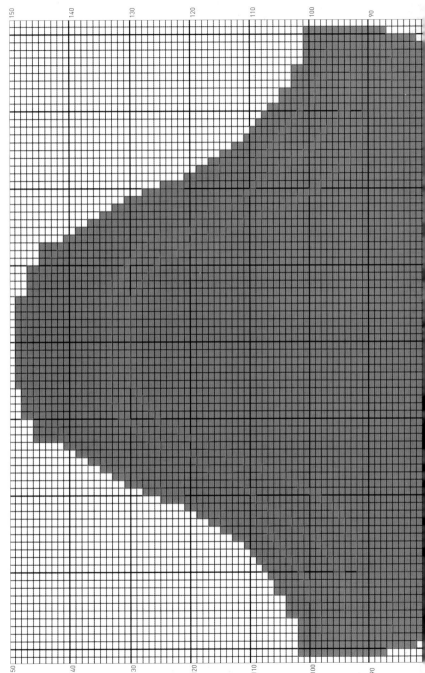

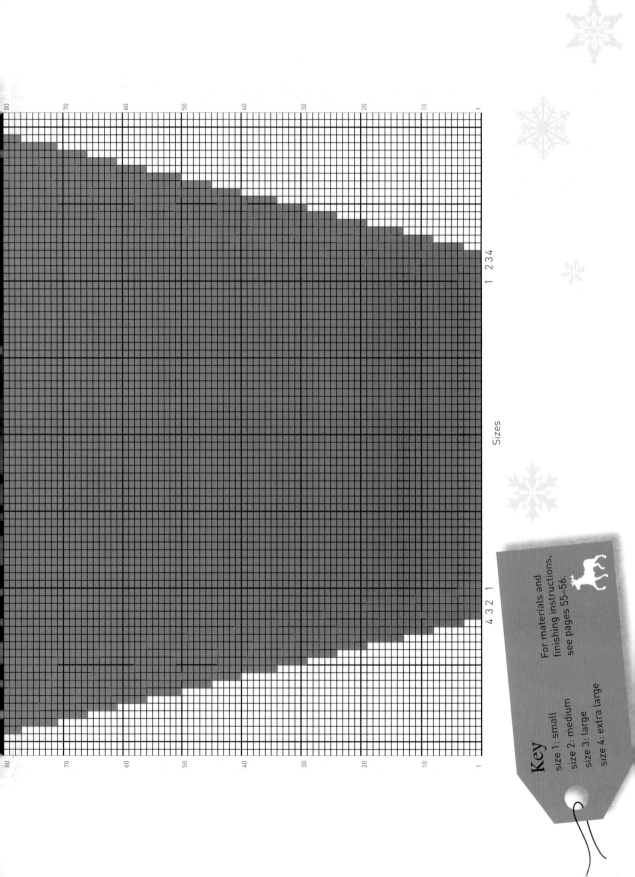

Sizes

1 2 3 4

4 3 2 1

Key

size 1: small
size 2: medium
size 3: large
size 4: extra large

For materials and
finishing instructions,
see pages 55–56.

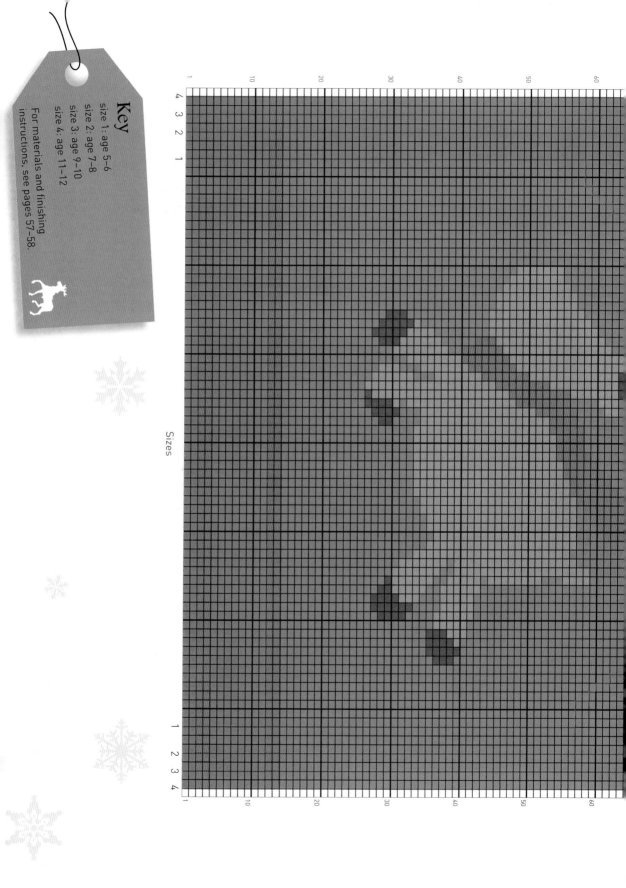

Key

size 1: age 5–6
size 2: age 7–8
size 3: age 9–10
size 4: age 11–12

For materials and finishing
instructions, see pages 57–58.

Sizes

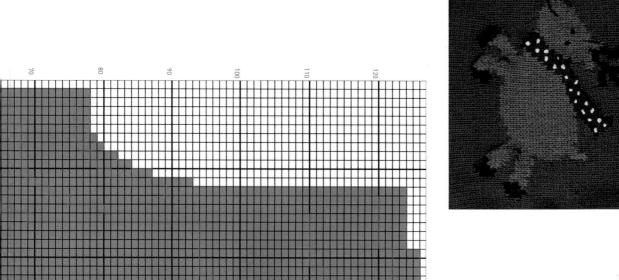

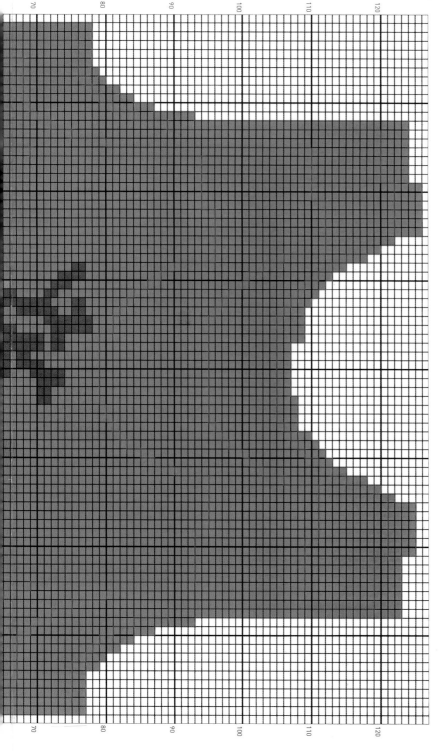

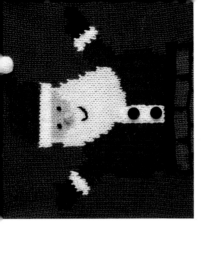

24 Santa Claus: CHILD FRONT

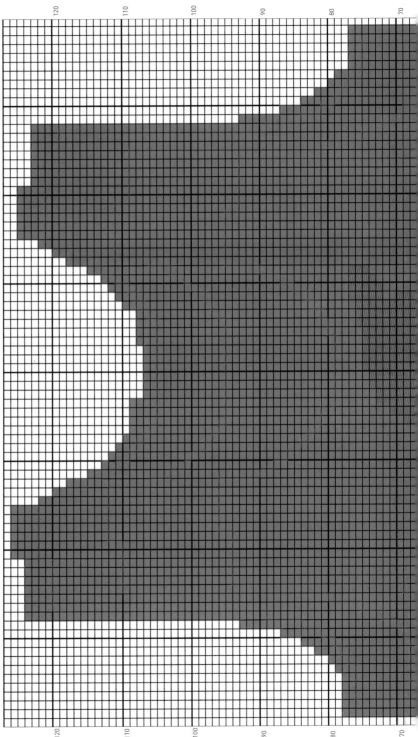

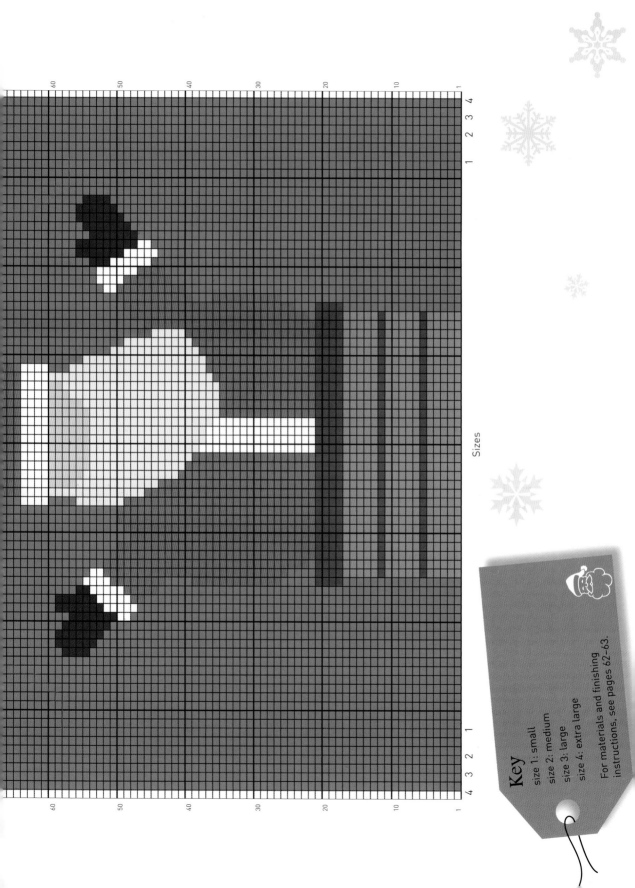

Sizes

Key

size 1: small
size 2: medium
size 3: large
size 4: extra large

For materials and finishing
instructions, see pages 62–63.

instructions on how to finish each of the sweater designs with surface embroidery; the materials you need for the motifs and close-up photographs of the designs. You will also find details of the charts you need, which are on the fold-out pages in the centre of the book. These can be removed or photocopied for easy reference and used alongside the basic sweater patterns on pages 16–31.

Child sweaters

Snowman, page 37

Winter Trees, page 41

Nordic Fair Isle, page 44

Christmas Pudding, page 50

Reindeer, page 57

Santa Claus, page 62

Snowman

This traditional snowman motif is knitted in cream against a light blue background with a contrasting red hat and spotty scarf, but you can knit this sweater in whichever colours you like. The cute little robin on the back of each sweater makes this design extra special. Use the intarsia technique for the colourwork (see page 12).

Adult motif
(charts 1 and 2)

Finishing instructions

Nose

Using orange yarn and 4.5mm (UK 7, US 7) needles, cast on 3 sts and purl 1 row.

Next row: (K1, M1) twice, K1 [5 sts].

Next row: P1, M1, P3, M1, P1 [7 sts].

Work 6 rows in SS.

Next row: K1, ssK, K1, K2tog, K1 [5 sts].

Next row: P1, sl1, P2tog, psso, P1 [3 sts].

Knit 1 row.

Cast off, leaving a long yarn end for finishing.

Buttons (make three)

Using black yarn and 4.5mm (UK 7, US 7) needles, cast on 1 st.

Next row: Kfbf [3 sts].

Work 3 rows in SS.

Next row: sl1, K2tog, psso [1 st].

Fasten off rem st. Leave a long yarn end for attaching the button to the snowman.

Materials for motif

80m (90yds) of 10-ply (Aran) yarn in each of the following colours: cream, red and mid-brown

50m (60yds) of 4-ply (fingering) yarn in sparkly white (use this yarn double when knitting)

Small amounts of black, orange and dark brown 10-ply (Aran) yarn for embroidery

Small amount of toy filling

The cute robin gives an eye-catching finishing touch to this cute sweater.

35

Bobble for snowman's hat

Using a double strand of sparkly white yarn, cast on 3 sts and purl 1 row.

Next row: (K1, M1) twice, K1 [5 sts].

Next row: P1, M1, P3, M1, P1 [7 sts].

Next row: K1, M1, K5, M1, K1 [9 sts].

Work 4 rows in SS.

Next row: K1, ssK, K3, K2tog, K1 [7 sts].

Next row: P1, P2tog, P1, P2togtbl, P1 [5 sts].

Next row: ssK, K1, K2tog [3 sts].

Cast off, leaving a long yarn end for finishing.

Front finishing

1. Run a length of yarn around the edge sts of the nose and gather slightly. Place a little toy filling inside. Sew to the snowman's face using the picture shown left as a guide.

2. Using the black yarn, embroider each eye with a French knot and the mouth using stem stitch.

3. Use a single strand of the sparkly white yarn to embroider French knots randomly on the snowman's scarf.

4. Place the three black knitted buttons on the front of the snowman, evenly spaced, and sew them into place.

5. Using dark brown yarn, embroider the snowman's arms using chain stitch.

6. Run a length of yarn around the edge sts of the white bobble and gather slightly. Place a little toy filling inside. Position the bobble on the snowman's hat using the picture as a guide and sew it into place.

Adult front motif

Back finishing

With black yarn, embroider the robin's legs using chain stitch and his eye using a single French knot. Embroider the beak using straight stitches worked in orange yarn.

Adult back motif

Child motif (charts 3 and 4)

Finishing instructions

Nose

Using orange yarn and 4.5mm (UK 7, US 7) needles, cast on 3 sts and purl 1 row.

Next row: (K1, M1) twice, K1 [5 sts].

Starting with a purl row, work 5 rows in SS.

Next row: K1, sl1, K2tog, psso, K1 [3 sts].

Purl 1 row.

Cast off, leaving a long yarn end for finishing.

Buttons (make three)

Using black yarn and 4.5mm (UK 7, l needles, cast on 1 st.

Next row: Kfbf [3 sts].

Work 3 rows in SS.

Next row: sl1, K2tog, psso [1 st].

Fasten off rem st, leaving a long yarn end for finishing.

Bobble for snowman's hat

Using a double strand of sparkly white yarn, cast on 3 sts and purl 1 row.

Next row: (K1, M1) twice, K1 [5 sts].

Next row: P1, M1, P3, M1, P1 [7 sts].

Work 4 rows in SS.

Next row: K1, ssK, K1, K2tog, K1 [5 sts].

Next row: P2tog, P1, P2togtbl [3 sts].

Cast off, leaving a long yarn end for finishing.

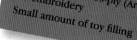

Materials for motif

80m (90yds) of 10-ply (Aran) yarn in each of the following colours: cream, red and mid-brown

50m (60yds) of 4-ply (fingering) yarn in sparkly white (use this yarn double when knitting)

Small amounts of black, orange and dark brown 10-ply (Aran) yarn for embroidery

Small amount of toy filling

Child front motif

Front finishing

1. Run a length of yarn around the edge sts of the nose and gather slightly. Place a little toy filling inside. Sew to the snowman's face using the picture shown left as a guide to positioning.

2. Using the black yarn, embroider each eye with a French knot and the mouth using stem stitch.

3. Use a single strand of the sparkly white yarn to embroider French knots randomly on the snowman's scarf.

4. Place the three black buttons on the front of the snowman, evenly spaced, and sew them into place.

5. Using dark brown yarn, embroider the snowman's arms using chain stitch.

6. Run a length of yarn around the edge sts of the white bobble and gather slightly. Place a little toy filling inside. Position the bobble on the snowman's hat using the picture as a guide and sew it into place.

Child back motif

Back finishing

With black yarn, embroider the robin's legs using chain stitch and his eye using a single French knot. Embroider the beak using straight stitches worked in orange yarn.

Winter Trees

This classic winter design has been knitted in a dark blue, variegated yarn for a stunningly stylish finish, but it looks equally good whatever colours you use. This versatile sweater uses the Fair Isle technique, which is described on page 11.

Adult motif (charts 5–7)

Finishing instructions

If you prefer, the tiny stars across the top of the sweater can be embroidered on using the Swiss darning technique after knitting (see page 13).

Materials for motif
160m (180yds) of 10-ply (Aran) yarn in silver grey

Above: adult front and back tree design

Left: large star motif

Child motif (charts 8–10)

Finishing instructions

If you prefer, the tiny stars across the top of the sweater can be embroidered on using the Swiss darning technique after knitting (see page 13).

Materials for motif
80m (90yds) of 10-ply (Aran) yarn in silver grey

Child motif

Nordic Fair Isle

This fabulous Fair Isle design combines traditional Nordic design with the Christmas theme. On the child sweater, the Christmas trees are all topped with sparkly gold stars and each of the reindeer has a shiny red nose. The adult version has a more detailed design, and just one tree and one reindeer has been adorned for a more subtle effect. The Fair Isle technique is described on page 11.

Adult motif (charts 11–13)

Finishing instructions

Embroider a red French knot for the nose on one of the reindeer on the front of the sweater. Sew a gold star on the top of one Christmas tree using straight stitches.

Materials for motif

80m (90yds) of 10-ply (Aran) yarn in each of the following colours: red, mid-brown and pale green

160m (180yds) of 10-ply (Aran) yarn in cream

Small amount of gold yarn for embroidery

Adult motif

Child motif (charts 14–16)

Finishing instructions

Embroider a red French knot for the nose of each of the reindeer. Sew gold stars on each of the Christmas trees using straight stitches.

Materials for motif

1 x 50g ball of 10-ply (Aran) yarn in each of the following colours: red, mid-brown, pale green and cream
Small amount of gold yarn for embroidery

Child motif

Christmas Pudding

The traditional British Christmas pudding is the basis of this fun festive design – make one for every member of the family for an extra special Christmas treat! Unlike the other designs in this book, the Christmas Pudding is knitted separately then stitched on to the front of the sweater – ideal for those who are less confident with colourwork. You can even knit the holly leaves separately and sew them on to the borders, meaning no colourwork at all! The patterns for the adult and child versions are provided on pages 46–52.

Tip
Make some cute matching hair bobbles using the pattern on page 53.

Adult motif (chart 17)

Christmas pudding instructions

Pudding

Using tweed-brown yarn and 4.5mm (UK 7, US 7) needles, cast on 19 sts and knit 1 row.

Purl 1 row.

Cast on 3 sts at beg of next 4 rows [31 sts].

Next row: K1, M1, K to last st, M1, K1 [33 sts].

Next row: P1, M1, P to last st, M1, P1 [35 sts].

Rep last 2 rows once more [39 sts].

Knit 1 row.

Next row: P1, M1, P to last st, M1, P1 [41 sts].

Knit 1 row.

Next row: P1, M1, P to last st, M1, P1 [43 sts].

Next row: K1, M1, K to last st, M1, K1 [45 sts].

Purl 1 row.

Next row: K1, M1, K to last st, M1, K1 [47 sts].

Rep last 2 rows twice more [51 sts].

Work 3 rows in SS.

Next row: K1, M1, K to last st, M1, K1 [53 sts].

Work 3 rows in SS.

Rep last 4 rows once more [55 sts].

Next row: K1, M1, K to last st, M1, K1 [57 sts].

Starting with a purl row, work 17 rows in SS.

Cast off.

Icing

The icing is made in four parts, which are joined together as you knit them. Use a double strand of sparkly white yarn and 4.5mm (UK 7, US 7) needles throughout.

Part 1

Cast on 3 sts and knit 1 row.

Next row: Cast on 2 sts at beg of row, P2, M1, P1 [6 sts].

Next row: K to last st, M1, K1 [7 sts].

Purl 1 row.

Next row: K to last st, M1, K1 [8 sts].

Next row: P1, M1, P to end of row [9 sts].

Knit 1 row.

Rep last 2 rows 3 more times [12 sts].

Next row: P1, M1, P to end of row [13 sts].

Next row: K to last st, M1, K1 [14 sts].

Next row: Cast on 2 sts at beg of row, P to end of row [16 sts].

Cut yarn and slide sts on to a spare needle with WS facing.

Part 2

Cast on 2 sts and knit 1 row.

Next row: P1, M1, P1 [3 sts].

Next row: K1, M1, K to last st, M1, K1 [5 sts].

Purl 1 row.

Rep last 2 rows once more [7 sts].

Knit 1 row.

Next row: P1, M1, P to last st, M1, P1 [9 sts].

Work 2 rows in SS.

Next row: K to last st, M1, K1 [10 sts].

Next row: P to last st, M1, P1 [11 sts].

Knit 1 row.

Next row: P1, M1, P to last st, M1, P1 [13 sts].

Knit 1 row.

Purl across all sts, turn work and cast on 2 sts, turn work and purl across 16 sts from Part 1 [31 sts].

Next row: K to last st, M1, K1 [32 sts].

Purl across all sts.

Cut yarn and place sts on a spare needle with WS facing.

Part 3

Cast on 3 sts and knit 1 row.

Next row: P2, M1, P1 [4 sts].

Next row: K to last st, M1, K1 [5 sts].

Next row: P to last st, M1, P1 [6 sts].

Work 2 rows in SS.

Next row: K1, M1, K to last st, M1, K1 [8 sts].

Work 3 rows in SS.

Next row: K1, M1, K to end of row [9 sts].

Next row: P1, M1, P to end of row [10 sts].
Work 2 rows in SS.
Next row: K1, M1, K to last st, M1, K1 [12 sts].
Purl 1 row.
Next row: K to last st, M1, K1 [13 sts].
Cut yarn and place sts on a spare needle with WS facing.

Part 4
Cast on 3 sts and knit 1 row.
Next row: P2, M1, P1 [4 sts].
Next row: K to last st, M1, K1 [5 sts].
Purl 1 row.
Next row: K1, M1, K to last st, M1, K1 [7 sts].
Next row: P to last st, M1, P1 [8 sts].
Next row: K1, M1, K to end of row [9 sts].
Purl 1 row.
Next row: K1, M1, K to end of row [10 sts].
Next row: Cast on 2 sts at beg of row, purl to end of row, purl across sts from Part 3 [25 sts].

Working across all 25 sts:

Knit 1 row.

Next row: P to last st, M1, P1 [26 sts].

Next row: K1, M1, K to end of row [27 sts].

Purl across all sts, M1, purl across sts from Parts 1 and 2 [60 sts].

Work 4 rows in SS.

Next row: K1, ssK, K to last 3 sts, K2tog, K1 [58 sts].

Purl 1 row.

Rep last 2 rows 4 more times [50 sts].

Next row: K1, ssK, K to last 3 sts, K2tog, K1 [48 sts].

Next row: P1, P2tog, P to last 3 sts, P2togtbl, P1 [46 sts].

Knit 1 row.

Next row: P1, P2tog, P to last 3 sts, P2togtbl, P1 [44 sts].

Next row: K1, ssK, K to last 3 sts, K2tog, K1 [42 sts].

Purl 1 row.

Next row: K1, ssK, K to last 3 sts, K2tog, K1 [40 sts].

Next row: P1, P2tog, P to last 3 sts, P2togtbl, P1 [38 sts].

Rep last 2 rows twice more [30 sts].

Cast off 3 sts at beg of next 4 rows [18 sts].

Cast off 4 sts at beg of next 2 rows [10 sts].

Cast off rem 10 sts.

Holly leaves (make two)

Using dark green yarn and 4.5mm (UK 7, US 7) needles, cast on 3 sts.

Work 2 rows in SS.

***Next row:** (Kfb) 3 times [6 sts].

Next row: P3, M1, P3 [7 sts].

Next row: K3, M1, K1, M1, K3 [9 sts].

Purl 1 row.

Next row: Cast off 3 sts, K to end of row [6 sts].

Next row: Cast off 3 sts, P to end of row [3 sts].

Rep from * once more.

Knit 1 row.

Next row: sl1, P2tog, psso.

Fasten off rem st. Leave a long yarn end for finishing.

Holly berry for top of pudding

Using red yarn and 4.5mm (UK 7, US 7) needles, cast on 3 sts and purl 1 row.

Next row: (K1, M1) twice, K1 [5 sts].

Starting with a purl row, work 3 rows in SS.

Next row: K1, sl1, K2tog, psso, K1 [3 sts].

Next row: sl1, P2tog, psso [1 st].

Fasten off rem st, leaving a long yarn for finishing.

Red berries for edging (make as required)

Using red yarn and 4.5mm (UK 7, US 7) needles, cast on 1 st.

Row 1: Kfbf [3 sts].

Starting with a purl row, work 3 rows in SS.

Next row: sl1, K2tog, psso [1 st].

Fasten off rem st. Leave a long yarn end for finishing.

Finishing instructions

1. Pin the pudding in place on the front of the sweater. Lightly pin the icing on top to ensure it fits below the neckline. Remove the icing and sew around the edges of the pudding. Make sure you do not catch the back of the sweater in the stitching. Re-pin the icing and sew it in place.

2. Lightly press the holly leaves and sew them in place at the top of the Christmas pudding.

3. Run a length of yarn around the edge sts of the holly berry and gather slightly. Place a little toy filling inside. Sew it in place between the two holly leaves.

4. Using the dark brown yarn, embroider French knots randomly on the pudding.

5. Gather each berry bobble in the same way as the larger berry and sew one in the centre of each pair of holly leaves around the hem and cuffs of the sweater. Use the picture opposite as a guide.

Adult motif

Child motif (chart 17)

Christmas pudding instructions

Pudding

Using tweed brown yarn and 4.5mm (UK 7, US 7) needles, cast on 8 sts and purl 1 row.

Cast on 2 sts at beg of next 6 rows [20 sts].

Next row: K1, M1, K to last st, M1, K1 [22 sts].

Next row: P1, M1, P to last st, M1, P1 [24 sts].

Rep last 2 rows once more [28 sts].

Knit 1 row.

Next row: P1, M1, P to last st, M1, P1 [30 sts].

Next row: K1, M1, K to last st, M1, K1 [32 sts].

Work 3 rows in SS.

Next row: K1, M1, K to last st, M1, K1 [34 sts].

Purl 1 row.

Next row: K1, M1, K to last st, M1, K1 [36 sts].

Work 3 rows in SS.

Next row: K1, M1, K to last st, M1, K1 [38 sts].

Starting with a purl row, work 17 rows in SS.

Cast off.

Icing

The icing is made in four parts, which are joined together as you knit them. Use a double strand of sparkly white yarn and 4.5mm (UK 7, US 7) needles throughout.

Part 1

Cast on 2 sts and purl 1 row.

Next row: K1, M1, K1 [3 sts].

Next row: P1, M1, P1, M1, P1 [5 sts].

Work 2 rows in SS.

Next row: K1, M1, K3, M1, K1 [7 sts].

Purl 1 row.

Next row: K1, M1, K to last st, M1, K1 [9 sts].

Cut yarn and slide sts on to a spare needle with WS facing.

Part 2

Cast on 3 sts and purl 1 row.

Next row: K1, M1, K1, M1, K1 [5 sts].

Purl 1 row.

Next row: K1, M1, K to end of row [6 sts].

Purl 1 row.

Next row: K1, M1, K to last st, M1, K1 [8 sts].

Purl 1 row.

Next row: K to last st, M1, K1 [9 sts].

Purl across row, turn work, cast on 2 sts, turn work, purl across Part 1 sts [20 sts].

Work 2 rows in SS.

Next row: K1, M1, K to end of row [21 sts].

Cut yarn and place sts on a spare needle with WS facing.

Part 3

Cast on 4 sts and purl 1 row.

Next row: K to last st, M1, K1 [5 sts].

Next row: P to last st, M1, P1 [6 sts].

Rep last 2 rows once more [8 sts].

Work 2 rows in SS.

Next row: K1, M1, K to last st, M1, K1 [10 sts].

Work 3 rows in SS.

Next row: K1, M1, K to end of row [11 sts].

Work 2 rows in SS.

Next row: P to last st, M1, P1 [12 sts].

Next row: K to last st, M1, K1 [13 sts].

Purl 1 row.

Next row: K to last st, M1, K1 [14 sts].

Purl 1 row.

Next row: K1, M1, K to last st, M1, K1 [16 sts].

Purl 1 row.

Next row: K to last st, M1, K1 [17 sts].

Purl across all sts, turn work, cast on 2 sts, turn work, purl across 21 held sts from Parts 1 and 2. Cut yarn and place sts on a spare needle with WS facing [39 sts].

Materials for motif

80m (90yds) of 10-ply (Aran) yarn in each of the following colours: red, tweed-brown, dark brown and dark green

180m (200yds) of 4-ply (fingering) yarn in sparkly white (use this yarn double when knitting)

Small amount of toy filling

Part 4

Cast on 3 sts and purl 1 row.

Next row: Cast on 2 sts, knit to end of row [5 sts].

Next row: P to last st, M1, P1 [6 sts].

Next row: K to last st, M1, K1 [7 sts].

Next row: P to last st, M1, P1 [8 sts].

Knit 1 row.

Purl across all sts, M1, purl across 39 sts on holder [48 sts].

Work 4 rows in SS.

Next row: K1, ssK, K to last 3 sts, K2tog, K1 [46 sts].

Purl 1 row.

Next row: K1, ssK, K to last 3 sts, K2tog, K1 [44 sts].

Next row: P1, P2tog, purl to last 3 sts, P2togtbl, P1 [42 sts].

Knit 1 row.

Next row: P1, P2tog, P to last 3 sts, P2togtbl, P1 [40 sts].

Next row: K1, ssK, K to last 3 sts, K2tog, K1 [38 sts].

Next row: P1, P2tog, P to last 3 sts, P2togtbl, P1 [36 sts].

Work 2 rows in SS.

Cast off 2 sts at beg of next 2 rows [32 sts].

Next row: K1, ssK, K to last 3 sts, K2tog, K1 [30 sts].

Next row: P1, P2tog, P to last 3 sts, P2togtbl, P1 [28 sts].

Work 2 rows in SS.

Cast off 2 sts at beg of next 4 rows [20 sts].

Cast off 3 sts at beg of next 2 rows [14 sts].

Cast off rem 14 sts.

Holly leaves (make two)

Using dark green yarn and 4.5mm (UK 7, US 7) needles, cast on 3 sts.

Work 2 rows in SS.

*Next row: (Kfb) 3 times [6 sts].

Next row: P3, M1, P3 [7 sts].

Next row: Cast off 2 sts, K to end of row [5 sts].

Next row: Cast off 2 sts, P to end of row [3 sts].

Rep from * once more.

Next row: sl1, P2tog, psso.

Fasten off rem st. Leave a long yarn end for finishing.

Holly berry for top of pudding

Using red yarn and 4.5mm (UK 7, US 7) needles, cast on 3 sts and purl 1 row.

Next row: (K1, M1) twice, K1 [5 sts].

Starting with a purl row, work 3 rows in SS.

Next row: K1, sl1, K2tog, psso, K1 [3 sts].

Next row: sl1, P2tog, psso [1 st].

Fasten off rem st, leaving a long yarn end for finishing.

Red berries for edging (make as required)

Using red yarn and 4.5mm (UK 7, US 7) needles, cast on 1 st.

Next row: Kfbf [3 sts].

Starting with a purl row, work 3 rows in SS.

Next row: sl1, K2tog, psso [1 st].

Fasten off rem st, leaving a long yarn end for finishing.

Finishing instructions

1. Pin the pudding in place on the front of the sweater. Lightly pin the icing on top to ensure it fits below the neckline. Remove the icing and sew around the edges c the pudding. Make sure you do not catch the back of the sweater in the stitching. Re-pin the icing and sew it in place.

2. Lightly press the holly leaves and sew them in place at the top of the Christmas pudding.

3. Run a length of yarn around the edge sts of the holly berry and gather slightly. Place a little toy filling inside. Sew it in place between the two holly leaves.

4. Using the dark brown yarn, embroider French knots randomly on the pudding.

5. Gather each of the berry bobbles in the same way as the larger berry and sew one in the centre of each pair of holly leaves around the hem and cuffs of the sweater. Use the picture below as a guide.

Holly hair bobbles

These pretty hair accessories are easy to make and add a delightful finishing touch to a little girl's Christmas outfit.

Holly leaves (make two)

Using dark green yarn and 4.5mm (UK 7, US 7) needles, cast on 3 sts.

Work 2 rows in SS.

*Next row: (Kfb) 3 times [6 sts].

Next row: P3, M1, P3 [7 sts].

Next row: Cast off 2 sts, K to end of row [5 sts].

Next row: Cast off 2 sts, P to end of row [3 sts].

Rep from * once more.

Next row: sl1, P2tog, psso.

Fasten off rem st.

Holly berry

Using red yarn and 4.5mm (UK 7, US 7) needles, cast on 3 sts and purl 1 row.

Next row: (K1, M1) twice, K1 [5 sts].

Starting with a purl row, work 3 rows in SS.

Next row: K1, sl1, K2tog, psso, K1 [3 sts].

Next row: sl1, P2tog, psso [1 st].

Fasten off rem st.

Making up

Sew the holly leaves to the hair elastic, using the picture above right as a guide. Make sure they are secure. Sew the berry in between the two holly leaves.

Materials

Small amounts of 10-ply (Aran) yarn in red and dark green

Hair elastic or ponytail holder

Reindeer

These fun reindeer motifs, complete with bright red noses that Rudolph himself would be proud of, will brighten even the dullest winter's day. The adult version sports two jolly reindeer that extend round to the back of the sweater, while the simplified child's version has a single reindeer on the front. The coordinating border around the hem and cuffs adds a touch of style to this eye-catching sweater. For the colourwork, use the intarsia technique, which is described on page 12.

Adult motif (charts 18–20)

Finishing instructions

Nose (make two)

Using red yarn and 4.5mm (UK 7, US 7) needles, cast on 3 sts and purl 1 row.

Next row: (K1, M1) twice, K1 [5 sts].

Starting with a purl row, work 3 rows in SS.

Next row: K1, sl1, K2tog, psso, K1 [3 sts].

Next row: sl1, P2tog, psso [1 st].

Fasten off rem st, leaving a long yarn end for finishing.

Materials for motif

80m (90yds) of 10-ply (Aran) yarn in each of the following colours: red, mid-brown and dark brown

Small amount of toy filling

Small amounts of 4-ply (fingering) yarn in sparkly white and black for embroidery

Bobbles for edging (make as required)

Using red yarn and 4.5mm (UK 7, US 7) needles, cast on 1 st.

Row 1: Kfbf [3 sts].

Starting with a purl row, work 3 rows in SS.

Next row: sl1, K2tog, psso [1 st].

Fasten off rem st, leaving a long yarn end for finishing.

Finishing

1. Run a length of yarn around the dge sts of each nose and gather slightly. Place a little toy filling inside each one. Sew to each reindeer's face using the pictures here and on page 56 as your guide.
2. Using the black yarn, embroider the eyes on each reindeer using two French knots and the mouth using stem stitch.
3. Embroider French knots on the reindeers' scarves using a single strand of sparkly white yarn.
4. Gather each red bobble in the same way as the noses and pin them in place along the edgings on the front, back and sleeves. Space them out evenly. Sew them in place securely.

Above: Adult front motif

Left: Adult back motifs

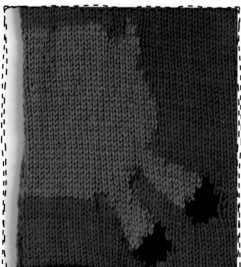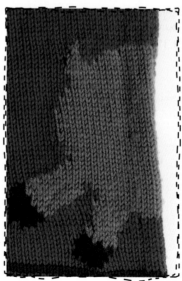

Child motif (charts 21 and 22)

Finishing instructions

Bobbles for reindeer's nose and edging (make as required)

Using red yarn and 4.5mm (UK 7, US 7) needles, cast on 1 st.

Row 1: Kfbf [3 sts].

Starting with a purl row, work 3 rows in SS.

Next row: sl1, K2tog, psso [1 st].

Fasten off rem st, leaving a long yarn end for finishing.

Finishing

1. Run a length of yarn around the edge sts of one of the red bobbles and gather slightly. Place a little toy filling inside. Sew it to the reindeer's face using the pictures here as a guide.

2. Using the black yarn, embroider the eyes on the reindeer using two French knots and the mouth using stem stitch.

3. Embroider French knots on the reindeer's scarf using a single strand of sparkly white yarn.

4. Gather each of the remaining bobbles in the same way as the reindeer's nose and pin them in place along the edgings on the front, back and sleeves. Space them out evenly. Sew them in place securely.

Materials for motif

80m (90yds) of 10-ply (Aran) yarn in each of the following colours: red, mid-brown and dark brown

Small amount of toy filling

Small amounts of 4-ply (fingering) yarn in sparkly white and black for embroidery

Child front motif

The Reindeer sweater and the Santa Claus sweater on the facing page make a great matching pair!

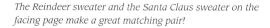

Santa Claus

An iconic Christmas motif, the jolly Santa Claus on the adult sweater
has been scaled down for the child's version. With no extra patterning
on the back or the sleeves, this is a good design to knit if you are a
relative beginner. Add real buttons and create knitted bobbles
for Santa's nose and the pompom on the
top of his hat. The sparkly white
yarn used for the trim on his coat and
hat add a touch of Christmas magic!
Use the intarsia technique
(see page 12) for the colourwork.

Adult motif (chart 23)

Finishing instructions

Nose

Using pale pink yarn and 4.5mm (UK 7, US 7) needles, cast on 3 sts and purl 1 row.

Next row: (K1, M1) twice, K1 [5 sts].

Next row: P1, M1, P3, M1, P1 [7 sts].

Work 3 rows in SS.

Next row: K1, ssK, K1, K2tog, K1 [5 sts].

Next row: K1, sl1, K2tog, psso, K1 [3 sts].

Purl 1 row.

Cast off, leaving a long yarn end for finishing.

Bobble for Santa's hat

Using a double strand of sparkly white yarn, cast on 3 sts and purl 1 row.

Next row: (K1, M1) twice, K1 [5 sts].

Next row: P1, M1, P3, M1, P1 [7 sts].

Next row: K1, M1, K5, M1, K1 [9 sts].

Work 4 rows in SS.

Next row: K1, ssK, K3, K2tog, K1 [7 sts].

Next row: P1, P2tog, P1, P2togtbl, P1 [5 sts].

Next row: ssK, K1, K2tog [3 sts].

Cast off, leaving a long yarn end for finishing.

Front finishing

1. Run a length of yarn around the edge sts of the nose and gather slightly. Place a little toy filling inside. Sew to Santa's face using the pictures here as a guide.

2. Using the black yarn, embroider each eye with a French knot and the mouth using stem stitch.

3. Place the two black buttons on the sparkly white strip on the front of the body and sew them in place.

4. Run a length of yarn around the edge sts of the white bobble and gather it slightly, as you did for the nose. Place some toy filling inside. Position the bobble on Santa's hat using the picture opposite as a guide and sew it into place.

5. Using dark brown yarn, embroider the vertical brick lines using chain stitch. Mark equal distances between the vertical brick lines with pins before sewing.

Materials for motif

80m (90yds) of 10-ply (Aran) yarn in each of the following colours: cream, red, mid-brown, dark brown, black and pale pink

180m (200yds) of 4-ply (fingering) yarn in sparkly white (use this yarn double when knitting)

Small amount of toy filling

Two 16mm (⅝in) black buttons

Adult motif

Child motif (chart 24)

Finishing instructions

Nose
Using pale pink yarn and 4.5mm (UK 7, US 7) needles, cast on 3 sts and purl 1 row.

Next row: (K1, M1) twice, K1 [5 sts].

Starting with a purl row, work 5 rows in SS.

Next row: K1, sl1, K2tog, psso, K1 [3 sts].

Purl 1 row.

Cast off, leaving a long yarn end for finishing.

Bobble for Santa's hat
Using a double strand of sparkly white yarn, cast on 3 sts and purl 1 row.

Next row: (K1, M1) twice, K1 [5 sts].

Next row: P1, M1, P3, M1, P1 [7 sts].

Work 4 rows in SS.

Next row: K1, ssK, K1, K2tog, K1 [5 sts].

Next row: P2tog, P1, P2togtbl [3 sts].

Cast off, leaving a long yarn end for finishing.

Front finishing
1. Run a length of yarn around the edge sts of the nose and gather slightly. Place a little toy filling inside. Sew to Santa's face using the picture, right, as a guide.

2. Using the black yarn, work a French knot for each eye and a curved line of stem stitch for the mouth.

3. Place the two black buttons on the sparkly white strip on the front of the body and sew them in place.

4. Run a length of yarn around the edge sts of the white bobble and gather it slightly, as you did for the nose. Place some toy filling inside. Position the bobble on Santa's hat using the photograph opposite as guidance and sew it into place.

5. Using dark brown yarn, embroider the vertical brick lines using chain stitch. Mark equal distances between the vertical brick lines using pins before sewing.

Materials for motif
80m (90yds) of 10-ply (Aran) yarn in each of the following colours: cream, red, mid-brown, dark brown, black and pale pink

180m (200yds) of 4-ply (fingering) yarn in sparkly white (use this yarn double when knitting)

Small amount of toy filling

Two 16mm (⅝in) black buttons

Child motif

Sizing charts

The child sweaters in this book are designed for ages 5–6, 7–8, 9–10 and 11–12. The adult sweater sizes are small, medium, large and extra large, and the equivalent adult sizes for men and women are provided in the first chart below. This is for guidance only, and the size you choose depends on the style you are looking for, whether it's tight and fitted or loose and baggy. I've therefore included two further charts giving the approximate dimensions of each sweater. These should provide all the information you need to knit the perfect Christmas sweater.

Approximate adult size equivalents

	Women (dress size)	Men (chest)
small	UK 8–10 (US 6–8)	81–86cm (32–34in)
medium	UK 12–14 (US 10–12)	91.5–96.5cm (36–38in)
large	UK 16–18 (US 14–16)	101.5–106.5cm (40–42in)
extra large	UK 20–22 (US 18–20)	112–117cm (44–46in)

Approximate dimensions of adult sweaters

	Chest width	Inside sleeve	Length to armhole
small	53cm (20¾in)	40.5cm (16in)	38cm (15in)
medium	56cm (22in)	40.5cm (16in)	39.5cm (15½in)
large	62cm (24½in)	40.5cm (16in)	39.5cm 15½in
extra large	64cm (25¼in)	42cm (16½in)	40.5cm (16in)

Approximate dimensions of child sweaters

	Chest width	Inside sleeve	Length to armhole
age 5–6	35.5cm (14in)	26.5cm (10½in)	24cm (9½in)
age 7–8	39.5cm (15½in)	29cm (11½in)	28cm (11in)
age 9–10	41cm (16¼in)	34cm (13½in)	30cm (11¾in)
age 11–12	43cm (17in)	36cm (14¼in)	33cm (13in)

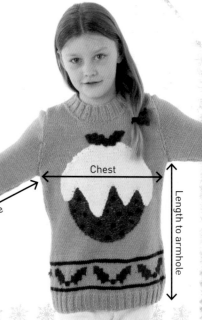

Chest

Inside sleeve

Length to armhole